Book Reviews

This book hits men where we live. Many men, and I was one of them, were never taught to be husbands and fathers; we tend to go at it without any real, fixed standards; even the successes seem to be primarily by accident. This book is designed to produce successes by intention.

C.E. Dickens has something vitally valuable to say – and says it plainly so we can understand it. He establishes himself in this book as a man of deep personal insight, deep spiritual values, and a great sensitivity to both husbands and fathers. He doesn't hesitate to share himself and his own family experiences in illustrating what he has to say.

This book is a book men will want to read and reread. I actually read and reread it myself. It's that loaded with practical and useable information. Both your mind and your heart will tell you this book is true.

Minister Aaron Williams
The Relationship Coach

This is an amazing read! I'm so grateful for this book, and I'll tell you why. So often we hear that there's no handbook for how to raise a child. I still believe that the Bible is the best resource for navigating through any situation in life. However, *Raising Cougars and Bears* will certainly give you a front row seat into the lives of ordinary people accomplishing extraordinary things. Thank you Mr. Dickens for being a living legacy and role model for many young families to come.

Viola Solomon
Director, Community Lending Mortgage

Raising Cougars and Bears (Parenting Daughters – A Father's Perspective); it is such a great, informative read. I enjoyed the fatherly perspective given on the subject of parenting. The level of transparency in Mr. Dickens' childhood upbringing, the correlation of cougars and bears, and the comparison of instinctive parenting to the interestingly intellectual nature of these dynamic creatures was nothing short of brilliant. The contractual agreement between parent and young adult....absolutely loved it. Certainly, a beautiful story told from a father with a big heart and business mind. Congratulations on yet another superb authoring project, it is certain to bless many!

Torsha Johnson
First Lady
Higher Dimension Church

On a daily basis while at work, I encounter men and fathers who would benefit from this impressive book. I was most intrigued by *Chapter 6 - Building a Core Foundation in the Home and Through Family Bonding*. I would strongly recommend *Raising Cougars and Bears (Parenting Daughters – A Father's Perspective)* to all young adult men, as well as young adult women. C. E. Dickens has produced a groundbreaking game changer and an insightful eye- opener for all who are impacted by the realities of current or future fatherhood.

Odis Lovell
Entrepreneur

A truly remarkable and well-crafted book. Wow! The author, C.E. Dickens has done it again! *Raising Cougars and Bears* captures the essence of the father-daughter relationship and how important this bond truly is as a young woman matures. The journey from child to womanhood is one best-traveled together, with parents having an active role in providing, leading and guiding. Using symbols from the animal kingdom, this work provides insight into how family (parent-child) dynamics and interactions plays a major role to lead to successful outcomes, versus disastrous and problematic circumstances.

Mr. Dickens provides with this masterpiece, a glimpse into the wonderfully complex and enduring responsibility of fathering good daughters. I recommend this book for parents looking for the hidden secrets of parenting. This parenting blueprint is touching, humorous at times and masterfully laid out. It is a must read. Mr. Dickens gives us the gift of knowledge and understanding in this beautiful, beautiful love story. Yes, a love story of a father standing in the gap to help ensure two basic needs – love and security are foundations of his daughters' destinies. This is a truly inspired work of genius.

Denise Kelly
Founder, dkjustaminute Ministry

This book, written by C.E. Dickens, describes the personal experiences of a father, as he raises two successful daughters, both of whom are currently pursuing post graduate studies. In this book, Mr. Dickens shares his positive and negative experiences of growing up in a single parent home as he emphasizes the importance of faith, love, and discipline in his life. As an adult, Mr. Dickens applies his values and strong moral compass to raising his own children to adulthood. The heartfelt message of the book is that a parent's presence and commitment to his children are the key necessities that enables their comfort and growth. *Raising Cougars and Bears* presents a rich array of suggestions that will benefit any parent to become a more responsible role model and loving care-giver to his children. I enjoyed reading this book very much, especially since it brought back many fond and fun memories of my own father as he guided me in my growth from childhood to adulthood.

Ba-Bie Teng, PhD
Professor of Molecular Medicine

Copyright © 2018 C.E. Dickens

All rights reserved

ISBN – 13: 978-1717143105

ISBN – 10: 1717143105

Cover foreground art created by:
Jocelyn Jones
High School Freshman
2018

Raising Cougars and Bears
(Parenting Daughters – A Father's Perspective)

As parents, specifically fathers, we must equip ourselves to meet the challenges associated with fatherhood into today's society. We must do so for the betterment and benefit of our daughters, their futures, society as a whole, and our legacies. My goal is to help young men who may contemplate becoming a father one day; to help young men who have already entered into fatherhood and; to help young women gain greater insight into understanding and helping the fathers of their future and current children so that they can become the best fathers (role models) they can be.

FOREWORD

Raising Cougars and Bears is for everyone that is a parent, an uncle, aunt, grandparent, or anyone who has the responsibility of rearing, mentoring, or caring for a child. That being said, this book, unfortunately, may not be for everyone. I know this appears to be a contradiction but bear with me, no pun intended. I will clear up any confusion about what I just said at the end of this foreword.

Calvin Dickens has written a masterful guide on how to successfully raise any child. Although his book is based on his own experiences of raising his daughters, the techniques, philosophies, and methods can be interchanged between raising both sons and daughters and actually transcends race. In his writing, Mr. Dickens has a clear, straight forward writing approach that is easy to follow and understand. Calvin draws on his personal experiences growing up as a child, dealing with an absentee father while providing statistical data to back up his positions. He also discusses topics that very few books dealing with fatherhood discuss, such as Legacy Building, Education, Love and Security, and most importantly the Importance of Faith and Biblical Principles.

When I began this foreword, I stated that this book is for everyone that is a parent, an uncle, aunt, grandparent, or anyone who has the responsibility of rearing, mentoring, or caring for a child. That being said, this book, unfortunately, will not be for everyone. While this book was written with the intended purpose to be a guide for Fatherhood, it deals just a much with the parent as it does with the child. Calvin Dickens confronts the problem of brokenness and unresolved issues that parents may have head-on. If the person attempting to raise a child has not dealt with their own childhood disappointments, hurts, insecurities, or brokenness they will continue the cycle of dysfunction and pass that same hurt and emptiness on to their children. This book forces you to hold up a mirror to your face and causes you to take a self-examination of oneself, both your mental and emotional state and your adaptability as a parent. Therefore, I caution all readers to stop reading at this point if you have not taken that honest self-evaluation. If not, then please do so before continuing on. If you choose to continue reading without taking that self-assessment, do not be surprised if you're unable to finish reading this wonderfully written guide due to its emotional depth and the powerful punch that it packs. That is why I stand by my statement that this guide is for everyone, but everyone will not be ready for it.

Homer L. Randle III

INTRODUCTION

I am a son of the deep, rural south. My foundation for *Raising Cougars and Bears (Parenting Daughters – A Father's Perspective)* began in a small town in the Florida Panhandle. After temporary living and working in Europe, Northeast Asia, and most of the continental United States, the in-home parental finish line is visible as fulfillment and achievement works its way towards raising two doctoral candidates; one in education (EdD) and the other as a medical doctor (MD).

I often chuckle when I hear people talk about the hood or housing projects, where they grew up. My neighborhood could have been considered "the hood of all hoods". My neighborhood was affectionately called River Bottom. Less than ¼ of a mile behind our home, there was a large, meandering river where raw sewage from the city's sewage treatment facility was consistently dumped into the river. For much of my youth, even though my neighborhood was located less than two miles from the county courthouse, the streets remained unpaved. The City cemetery was directly across the street. It was established around the year 1820. A limited number of African Americans were permitted to be buried there however, their plots were located in a small, rear area of the cemetery. The city's garbage disposal dump was less than ½ mile, up the hill from my house. Finally, a rendering plant was also located less than three football fields from my back door. A rendering plant is a processing operation where dead animals are recycled into products from human food to biodiesel. The remains and waste from slaughterhouses are the primary contributors to these facilities. There were days when the air quality was simply unbearable. As kids, while playing in the street, we had to regularly and temporarily suspend our games and activities to make way for the large trucks carrying trash or dead animal carcasses. Even though the current neighborhood has changed, buying a home in such an area today would be considered an environmental disaster if not environmental suicide.

Anyone, all of us are capable of rising above the challenges life has to offer so that we can achieve or be a catalyst for others to achieve something greater. Our challenges involve everything from ensuring our basic needs are met, through overcoming societal disparities to achieving fulfillment for ourselves and our children. Just like us, a parallel exist in the animal kingdom as its members also strive to overcome its daily challenges for survival.

As a man, I am typically drawn to observing the ways of the animal kingdom. I enjoy watching various episodes on the Discovery Channel, Wild Kingdom, Planet Earth and other similar outlets. I have discovered a well-established hypothesis; within that theory there is so much we can learn and gain from observing animals in their natural environment. Humans can gain insight on trusting your instincts, playing fair, respecting your elders, reaching your goals, perseverance, and living sustainably.

In acknowledgement of my daughters' undergraduate educational achievements from their colleges of choice, my oldest is a proud "Cougar" (University of Houston-established 1927) and my youngest is proud to be a "Bear" (Baylor University-chartered 1845). As for me, I am simply a proud (be all you can be) father. Hence, I chose to use the "Raising Cougars and Bears" title and metaphor to illustrate the significance education (formal and informal) plays as a cornerstone to raising healthy, happy, and successful children. My wife and I did not plan for our daughters to become cougars and bears, this was their decision. Once the decision was made, our job was to support them so they would be able to enjoy, learn, grow, and excel in their new academic environments. My daughters could have easily became eagles or tigers or any other well-known mascot commonly used by many of our great universities to promote spirit and pride. While acknowledging the possibility that there could have been a different title to this publication, the material and conceptual ideas would have remained unchanged.

As parents, not only do we want our children to survive but we also want our children to experience success. With that being said, success means different things to different people. Whatever success means to you and your family, I believe education is a conduit to success for our children. Education is the key to success because it opens doors for people of all backgrounds, and it expands the human mind with knowledge. The vast amount of knowledge gained through education prepares individuals to solve problems, teach others, earn a living, function at a higher level and implement transformational ideas. Without education, one's chances for securing a good job and ascending to a higher economic and social status are often limited.

Education is not limited to the classroom. Informal education also has significant value in educating our children. Informal education is simply those things you learn about outside of the classroom environment.

I also want to help dispel the stereotype of why daughters can't be raised to be independent, dynamic, and confident in striving to be whatever they want to be or do whatever it is they want to do. For the record, women are just as capable in any role of their choosing if or when ample opportunities are presented or if they simply choose to do so.

Raising children in today's society can be extremely challenging and demanding. And since I was blessed to be the father of girls, my parenting skills and perspective are naturally focused on girls. By no means do I mean to diminish the importance of rearing boys, I would wholeheartedly agree that rearing boys is just as demanding and challenging. As a result, the parenting challenges and practical solutions discussed in this publication are not limited to fathers and daughters but also includes sons, step-children, foster and adopted children. It doesn't matter if it's called a family, clan, tribe, or pride;

fathers are created to be providers, protectors, and leaders to those where a family bond is essential to overcoming life's challenges.

In this publication, I want to share my experiences as a father. I also want to highlight some of my failures and successes so that others may benefit from my experiences. The world in which "baby boomers' and generation X'ers (most fathers of today) grew up in is vastly different for millennials, generation Y, and generations of the future. As parents, more specifically fathers, we must equip ourselves to meet the challenges associated with fatherhood. We must do so for the betterment and benefit of our children, their futures, society as a whole, and our legacies.

Dedication

To my late mother, Ora M. Peterson, who courageously took on the role of mother and father; I am thankful to her for being a role model, demonstrating the true meaning of sacrifice, and teaching me how to appreciate and understand the value of a strong woman.

To my wife, Fanetta, the true love of my life who taught me how to love and appreciate a strong companion for life, my other conscience, my second heartbeat, and the ideal mother and role model to my daughters.

To my daughters, Camile and Latrice, who through your births, your lives, and your developing intellect, inspired me and positively changed my life forever.

And to my Pastor, Terrance H. Johnson (a.k.a. Pastor J.) and First Lady Torsha Johnson (a.k.a. Lady J.), my spiritual first family. Thank you for your support, trust, encouragement, and the various opportunities afforded me.

Special Dedication

To all of my lovely nieces who are like daughters to me. Thank you all for the love you have always shown me. To Sheryl, Simone, Sharonda (in memory of), Tabetha, Nevea, Tammy, Latisha, Sharondria, Rolanda, Tiffany, Roshanna, Franika, and Jazzmyn; I will always cherish our relationships.

To my sisters, Barbara and Sharron, I love you with all my heart and soul. Thank you for helping me to develop into the man I am today.

Table of Contents

Chapter	Page
Preface – What's That Connection Again Between Cougars and Bears	18
Chapter 1 – Fatherhood & Daddy, What Does It Mean?	22
Chapter 2 – Your Formative Years Will Influence the Way You Parent	30
Chapter 3 – The Impact of Marriage and Relation- on Co-Parenting, Single-Parenting, & Blended Families	38
Chapter 4 – Statistics & Data, What Do They Reveal? Why Are They So Important? Why Should We Care?	45
Chapter 5 – The Two Basic Needs: Love & Security	58
Chapter 6 – Building A Core Foundation In The Home & Through Family Bonding	71
Chapter 7 – Education, The Great Equalizer	81
Chapter 8 – The Transformation From Young To Young Women; Advice About Boys & Men	93
Chapter 9 – Building A Legacy	105
Chapter 10 – The Importance of Faith & Biblical Principles	114
That's a Wrap	125

Appendix 1 – Bilateral Contractual Agreement	127
Appendix 2 – Fatherhood Interview – Pastor Terrance H. Johnson	133
Appendix 3 – Fatherhood Interview – Counselor Aaron Williams	135
A Quick Review	140
References	141
Author's Bio	143

It is often said, "A picture is worth a thousand words". The photograph above was taken at a Houston Astros game during a Father's Day Celebration with my daughters. Considering all of the available photographs in the family archives, this particular one best captures the true essence of the father/daughter relationship.

The message behind the photograph is an expression of love for one another by spending quality time together and foregoing what you may not like for the benefit of others. Buying gifts and things have a place in father/daughter relationships but spending memorable and quality time together is priceless.

PREFACE

What's That Connection Again between Cougars and Bears?

Cougars - The largest of the small cat species, these *agile* animals can jump up to 20 feet from the ground into a tree. Agility isn't the cougar's only defining characteristic -- these *perceptive* cats are skilled hunters and *masters of communication*. As solitary cats, cougars don't often interact with each other unless mating or child-rearing; however, they are *skilled at the art of communication*. Cougars leave messages for each other in the form of urine and feces markings as well as deep scratches on trees. This is their way of delineating territory without coming face-to-face. Cougars are *powerfully* built, agile hunters. Their hind legs are more muscular than their front legs and give them tremendous jumping power. Their *flexible* spines and quick speed afford these cats the ability to *change directions* in a flash, essential for both ambushing and chasing prey. Cougars quietly stalk their prey, then leap at close range for attack; however, they also have to be ready for a chase if an agile food source makes a run for it.

Bears - Bears are highly evolved social animals with *intelligence* comparable to that of the great apes. Bears often share friendship, resources and security. They *form hierarchies* and have *structured kinship* relationships. Bears are very *strong* and *powerful* animals. Bears are not mean or malicious; they are very gentle and tolerant animals. Mother bears are affectionate, protective, devoted, strict, sensitive and attentive with their young. Not unlike people, bears can be empathetic, fearful, joyful, playful, social and even altruistic. They're all individuals and have *unique personalities*. Cubs, as well as older bears, engage in social play and have ritualistic mechanisms to meet strangers and decide if they are friendly or not. Bears routinely distinguish between threatening and non-threatening human behavior. Bears *communicate* using body language, sounds and smells. Bears treat humans just as they would other bears; the problem is that bears are very physical with each other, with the intentional use of bites, swats or body posturing.

Even though cougars and bears are considered of the same animal species, they are distinctly different. Similarly, if you are privileged to become the father of more than one child, you will soon discover that each child's personality is also distinctly different. While the family bloodlines may be the same, the make-up of each sibling is individually unique.

The thought of future Chief Executive Officers, managers at various levels in the workplace, politicians, athletes, sports officials, scientist, engineers, surgeons, military service members, law enforcement, firemen, pilots, truck drivers, carpenters, mechanics, and etc. usually conjures up visions of male-dominated professions. To help prepare our daughters to be all they can be requires everyone to think non-traditionally, outside of the box. This nontraditional, outside of the box approach may require fathers and daughters to take on (somewhat of a non-traditional) approach or re-adjust their thinking to help fulfill their goals and dreams.

I want to reinforce the importance of a supporting family environment and how education ultimately impacts our children. To be fully independent, young women must be taught in ways that will help hone and develop the necessary skills to survive and thrive in our modern-day society. The developing skill sets that I am referring to are not foreign to us; attributes and characteristics such as intelligence, communication, agility, flexibility, understanding power, identifying potential threats, providing, protecting, operating within a hierarchy, instinctual abilities, and on and on. That means developing a skill set that may often appear similar to members of the animal kingdom, including cougars and bears. We don't want our daughters to abandon the way God created them or their God-given purpose, we do however want them to be fully prepared to flourish in any environment of their choosing. This publication provides practical insights into establishing the necessary foundation to raising independent, dynamic, and confident daughters.

What Are Little Girls Made of?

Nursery Rhyme

What are little boys made of?
What are little boys made of? Frogs and snails, And puppy-dogs' tails; That's what little boys are made of.

What are little girls made of?
What are little girls made of?
Sugar and spice,
And all that's nice;
That's what little girls are made of.

Chapter 1 – Fatherhood and Daddy, What Does It Mean?

> *I have had two successful careers but, without a doubt, the most important job title I have ever had is the job title of "Daddy"*

One mandatory item on every man's bucket list should be to witness the birth of his children. I am not going to discuss any further and risk understating exactly how crucial witnessing the birth of your child is except to say, once witnessed, your life will be positively changed, forever.

So, what does it mean to be a father? A Father is one who leads. A Father is a provider. A protector. A father is someone who handles all of his responsibilities. A father is a mentor to his children. A father is a role model. A father knows how and when to show love and compassion. A father also knows how and when to discipline with love. A father is someone who is true to his faith. A father offers encouragement. A father does what he says he will do, when he says he'll do it. A father's life changes forever if he is fortunate enough to see you enter into this world at the time of birth.

Dads are heroes. Dads help make dreams come true. Dads don't have to say much when they are displeased about something; somehow "that look" is instinctively conveyed. Dads sometimes elicit feelings of goofiness and embarrassment from their daughters. Dads fix things. Dads make boyfriends feel uncomfortable. Dads can be like pack mules when vacationing or when transporting their precious cargo to the freshman dorm. Dads are also known as ATM machines. Dads give non-official driving lessons. Dads can sometimes appear repetitive by bragging about how things were back in the day. Dads are a little squeamish if he has to transport you to the emergency room. Dads take advice about what does or does not look cool about his attire. Dads plan fun stuff. Dads are tough until their little girls pleading eyes places a gaping hole in their hearts, like an unavoidable laser. Dads cannot stand to see girls cry.

Even though father and dad have technically different meanings, for the purpose of this project, I have decided to use the terms interchangeably. A father is a reproductive term referring to the male biological parent of a child. A dad is a male parental figure that is present and participating in a child's life.

Fatherhood is the kinship relation between an offspring and the father. This involves doing whatever it takes for your child(ren) and your home to grow, develop, and prosper; receive teachings, security, safety, and love. Fatherhood is accepting full responsibility for another life.

When my wife told me she was pregnant with our first child, this news was very special to me for two reasons. One, I knew she very much wanted to experience motherhood. I may have been okay with not having children but my wife may have felt a void if we didn't have children. Secondly, prior to the news of my wife's pending pregnancy, we had been married for six years. During the initial six years of marriage, we tried to conceive for four of those years. Once the news sunk in, I had a myriad of feelings. I felt anxiety, happiness, pride, hope, thankfulness, and even fear. The fear involved sailing in the unchartered waters of fatherhood.

For two years and seven months, I adjusted to the challenges of fatherhood. It was during this time my wife gave me an update on our growing family. Our second daughter was not planned. My wife says I was more nervous about the second pregnancy than I was about the first. Excluding medical concerns, maybe the pressure was beginning to sink in about responsibility. This is the point where the realities of fatherhood really began to impact me. The weight of husband, father, provider, protector, leader, career, and security for a wife and two children began to take its grip. After dealing with those emotions, my love for my wife, my firstborn, and my soon to be born second daughter began to manifest itself. At that point, my instincts began to kick in, I knew I had to bear down, buckle the chin strap, and do what was expected as a result of my newfound status of being daddy to two girls. It was time to be a real man, a father.

Some may argue that it is difficult for a woman to teach a boy how to become a man while likewise it is just as difficult for a man to teach a girl how to become a woman. Ideally, I would suggest, having both a male and female parental role model, no matter the child's gender, contributes wholesomely to the overall well-roundedness of the child.

We know in life, what is ideal is not always our reality. I think very few would argue against how important it is today that parents need to go the extra mile to ensure that when your child departs from you, they are fully prepared to meet the challenges presented to them by our modern day society.

Make no mistake about it, there are distinct roles for fathers and mothers. Mothers are nurturers, comforters, instinctive, caring, and they help fulfill emotional needs while also demonstrating many other valuable traits, characteristics and contributions. However, don't get the roles of fathers and mothers confused. I have also discovered that the child knows the distinct difference between the two parental roles. I also believe that this distinction is actually healthy for the family unit. You can probably cross reference this claim with the experts, I'm confident there's research to support this claim.

An exclusive TODAY survey of 2,000 moms and dads shows that fathers are more involved than ever before with their children, both emotionally and practically. While moms increasingly share the responsibility for the family's income, dads are assisting with more of the childcare and household chores. As we know it, traditional father/mother roles are changing. According to the survey, about 75 percent of fathers say being a dad is their most important job, and 61 percent of dads say they are more involved with their children than their father was with them.

I often joke with my wife by telling her, I'm the Chief Executive Officer (CEO) and she's the Chief Operating Officer (COO) and/or the Chief Financial Officer (CFO). I'm engaged primarily in the overall strategic decisions and she's more engaged in the day-to-day operational decisions. When sound advice is needed or parenting decisions must be made, usually before we fall asleep or when dining alone, we are all ears and have each other's undivided attention. I soon discovered however, there are situations and occasions where I had to abandon the CEO role and roll up my sleeves to deal with everyday life issues. Oftentimes, every day, life issues are unavoidable and require your undivided attention.

As a father, when you lead, provide, and protect, it goes without saying, it is impossible to do so without a job! Job, meaning stable and consistent employment. It makes no difference if your job is working in a fast food restaurant or corporate America. As a provider you do what you have to do. Unless you are mentally or physically disabled, what excuse do you have? Starting out, you may not work in the job of your dreams but you've got to do whatever you have got to do until a better opportunity presents itself. Just let me add, doing illegal, entrepreneurial type work does not count. If something were to go wrong, you definitely would not be in a position to lead, provide, and protect.

My wife and I discussed the possibility of a third child, trying for that boy. After much debate, I was able to convince her that I was happy being blessed with two girls. My rationale was if I am going to give fatherhood my maximum effort, two children would place me in a better position to be all I could be as a father. Even though at the time of our debate, I was not aware of or had access to pertinent facts and figures about parenthood. According to a recent report released by the Department of Agriculture, a middle income, married couple with two children was expected to spend $233,610 to raise a child in 2015. And that number only covered the cost from birth to age 17, it did not include college expenses. Families can expect to spend between $12,350 and nearly $14,000 a year on average to raise a child.

I believe for many men, the opportunity to provide for the ones you love is critical to self-worth and self value. I also believe your job is the one area of life where the biggest fathering sacrifices are made. As I reflect on the early "grinding" stages of work, the grind was not about me; it was about those who were depending on me. There were days, there were situations where under normal circumstances, I probably would not have endured. But when you accept the fact that others are depending on you, you find a way to overcome. While we are on the subject of jobs, don't be disappointed if she (your wife or daughter's mother) makes more money than you do; at the end of the day, your daughter benefits. Be proud of yourself, that you were able to attract a woman with a high income status. Not only that, use your lesser paying job situation as an incentive to improve yourself; I've always taken pleasure in proving others wrong. When you say I can't, I'm determined to show you I can.

For me, it is important that before you can fully understand the true meaning of fatherhood, you must first understand the true meaning of manhood. As a youngster and maturing young man, I routinely observed and spent time with a few older males. As I observed them, there were little take-a-ways, certain characteristics about them that

I admired or was inspired by. As an example, one neighborhood senior citizen with limited education, who was the local checkers champion, taught me that even though you may be the master of your craft, always take the time to help develop others. In later years, another gentleman, easily 25 years senior to me was well respected by many people; he had two successful careers and had been married for 50 (+) years. This gentleman taught me the significance of being a role model, humbleness, and how to lead by a firm but quiet and respectful example.

If at all possible, prior to becoming a father, get to know and understand self first, establish job security and develop your spiritual maturity. Before you can successfully take on the rigors of fatherhood, you must exert time, energy, and effort into investing in you. If armed with this foundation, it will surely make your transition into fatherhood so much easier.

Fatherhood thoughts (in general):

- Never disrespect your wife or daughter's mother in front of your daughter
- Be a teacher and mentor to your children
- Keep all promises
- Be an example and a role model
- Encourage and motivate
- Learn how to say I'm sorry where appropriate
- Listen to sound advice; find a mentor or accountability partner for yourself
- Whatever you do as a father, never show favoritism over one child versus the other; stepchildren and adopted children included
- Fatherhood is the perfect time to start setting aside ego, pride, selfishness, and an "it's all about me" mentality
- I would submit to you that before you can successfully lead others, you must first be able to successfully lead yourself

- As fathers, oftentimes the public persona we portray does not match up with the private reality; if true, let's work on that.
- Model the behavior you want others to emulate

Oftentimes as fathers, we do not excel at expressing ourselves with words. What do we do when struggling with this issue? Could it be that as boys, we were taught to be tough, hard, and not to express or show our emotions? First, recognize the fact that this is an area of your life where improvement is needed. Secondly, make a concerted effort to do something about it. Finally, reach out to family and loved ones to offer up an assist. Daughters will typically and easily help you overcome this perceived barrier, if you simply let them.

In my first career, I was a career soldier. As a career soldier, routine smiling was not part of the job description. Showing emotions or wearing your emotions on your sleeve (as we used to say) was not conducive to preparing for war. Displaying a serious and no-nonsense demeanor was part of the military culture, particularly as a leader. Well, having girls high jacked that particular thinking process. Close family members who obviously have known me all their lives were amazed at the transformation I had made once my daughters were born. Having daughters softened me up; took the edge off; offered a different outlook on life. The truth is this change, this transformation was good for me and I knew it. Not only did I benefit personally from learning to be a more tolerant dad (overall) but this also helped me in my second career as an Operations Manager at a busy airport. My level of sensitivity towards dealing with customers, my employees and others can be indirectly attributed to my daughters. Your "taking the edge off" experience may not be as drastic as mine however, I definitely benefitted in my development as a man because of my experience of being a father to daughters.

"A daughter may outgrow your lap, but she will never outgrow your heart".
—Author Unknown—

"We need fathers to realize that what makes you a man is not the ability to have a child, it's the courage to raise one."

—President Barak Obama—

Things to Build On:

- Make no mistake about it, there are well defined roles for fathers and mothers. The child knows the distinct difference between the two parental roles.
- For me, it is important that before you can fully understand the true meaning of fatherhood, you must first understand the true meaning of manhood.
- If at all possible, prior to becoming a father, get to know and understand yourself first, establish job security and develop your spiritual maturity. Before you can successfully take on the rigors of fatherhood, you must exert time, energy, and effort into investing in you.
- As fathers, oftentimes the public persona we portray does not match up with the private reality; if true, let's work on that.
- Model the behavior you want others to emulate

Chapter 2 - Your Formative Years Will Influence the Way You "Parent"

> *During the teenage and young adult (before fatherhood) years, men are not necessarily focused as much as we should be on risk, consequences, potentially harmful behavior, and the possibility of hurting others.*

Without a doubt, the most important parenting influence on me was my late Mother. The second most important parenting influence on me was growing up in a single parent, household. The fact that my father, grandfather, or any other male within my immediate family were not part of my life definitely impacted me. I could have very easily become a "statistic" but by the grace of God, I survived. Statistics back this up. Males, particularly African American males who grow up in households where there is no father or male role model are more inclined to fail or become part of the Juvenile Justice System. Even though there was no in-house father figure, I was able to take a negative situation and turn it into a positive. Early in my life, I made a vow that if I ever had children, I would do everything within my power to be there for them. You see, I wanted to ensure that my children were able to have what I did not have. Also, during my upbringing, a sense of responsibility had been ingrained in me. So much credit for my early development goes to my late mother. As I reflect back on my childhood, I wasn't too bad of a child but I could have been better. I can recall my mother teaching me about accountability and responsibility. As an example, I can recall her driving around in the car, stopping at several places where she had a running credit account. Sorry, there were no credit cards at that time and if there were, we didn't have any. She would drive up outside, give me specific instructions on what to do and say, as she allowed me to go inside to make a payment on her credit. I would tell the owner who I was, what I was there for, and how much I wanted to pay. By the way, I had to return with a receipt. As I reflect on these encounters much later in life, I began to realize exactly how my mother had started the process of molding and shaping me to engage others from a business perspective, while training me on the importance of paying bills, maintaining good credit, assuming accountability and responsibility.

As a result of my late mother's influence, I also learned how to deal with females very early in life; having two older sisters also enhanced the female influence on me. As you might imagine, having a Mother as a single provider meant she had to be tough, independent, strong, and a women of immense faith. Naturally, as I matured, I had no problem dealing with strong, independent women. Needless to say, I married a strong and independent woman and we tried to raise our daughters to be strong and independent.

Since there were only a few male role models in the neighborhood, the next best place to look for them was in church. Thankfully, there were several men in the church who were excellent role models. This was not a direct hands on experience however; so much was gained from a distance as I watched these men as they went about performing their church duties and responsibilities. These men were all deacons. They were distinguished and respected. They led by example. They practiced "servant leadership". Outside of performing their church-related duties and responsibilities, they all were generally really soft spoken men.

While playing sports, I did not feel as if the coaches had my best interest in mind. Also, there were a limited number of male relatives to lean on. The few male relatives that were there were not in a position to focus a lot of time on helping to develop someone else's child. As a result of this void of not having males to bond with or teach me, for the most part, I had to turn inwardly. This revelation is not intended to reflect negativity, this is just the way it was back then.

Even though my late mother was limited in education, in fact, she had a 9th grade education, I do recall her being passionate about three things concerning the rearing of her children. One, she had experienced and witnessed the hardships of premature pregnancies and she did not want her daughters to fall into the same trap. Secondly, she fought hard to prevent her sons, me in particular, from falling into the juvenile delinquent trap. Thirdly, she was serious about sharing her faith. Her methods of getting her point across may have been direct but I know now, it was done out of love and a deep-rooted desire to see her children rise above perceived disadvantages and become successful in life.

As odd as it may sound, during my adolescence, I thought growing up without a father was normal. I grew to accept it as "that's just the way it was". I had every opportunity in the world to use this as an excuse to fail. Rather than use my reality as a crutch, I decided early in life to use this as a motivator. At an early age, I made up in my mind that if or when I had children, I would be there for them. Most of the homes in the neighborhood I grew up in were a microcosm of my home situation. Easily, 75% of the homes in my neighborhood had a female as head of household. Connecting the dots, the females within this community help raise and remain watchful over children other than their own. We've all heard the saying, "It takes a village to raise a child"; it's true, I am a product of a village. Fast forward to today, the neighborhood village concept may not be the same, however, that modern-day village is more inclined to be family and extended family. The concept remains the same, you cannot successfully parent alone. A support group is needed along the way to provide support.

With a name like River Bottom, my neighborhood was not known for producing success stories. In my mind, River bottom was considered a notch or two below the projects. Among other things, a meandering river flowed behind our house where the city's sewage treatment plant often dumped raw sewage into the river. I now realize there are benefits of having to start life from the so called bottom; benefits of having to scratch and claw your way to rise above hardships. When life demands you re-visit adversity, you don't become unglued; overcoming adversity becomes instinctual or ingrained into your personal problem-solving thought process.

My upbringing experiences are different from your experiences and your life experiences are different from mine. Have you ever asked yourself, "Why do I think the way I do"? What influences on my life helped shape me the way I am shaped? Was there stability in your home? Was love openly expressed? Did you have an absentee father or mother? Did you witness verbal and physical abuse? Did you watch your parents endure an ugly divorce? Did your family struggle to pay bills? Was your family forced to move from one location to another to overcome financial difficulties? Did your parent(s) have an opportunity to support your extra-curricular activities? Did you endure bullying? Did your family have to make a choice between needs versus wants? Was a dear family member struggling with drug use? Was going to church a part of the regular family routine? Did your family ever pray together? Did you suffer the loss of a love one at an early age? Have you ever wondered, how can I become a better man? How can I become a better father? These issue and more can have a profound impact on you and your parenting skills. Do not be afraid to recognize the situation for what it truly is. If chains need to be broken, strive to break the chain. If breaking the chains includes seeking professional help, do what you know is best for you and your family. Do not allow your issues to be passed on to the next generation.

In the passage of life, particularly as I've moved on to the golden years (middle-age and beyond), it simply amazes me how a man's focus on dating and female relationships in general, shifts from one mindset during the teenage and young adult years, to a completely different mindset once fatherhood is encountered. During the teenage and young adult (before fatherhood) years, men are not necessarily as focused as we should be on risk, consequences, potentially harmful behavior, and the possibility of hurting others. Miraculously, as soon as fatherhood is experienced, oftentimes men become protective of the values that we were previously reckless with. As I have advanced in age and grown in maturity, I have tried to warn young men of how impactful youthful indiscretions can be. Oftentimes, we are living in the moment and not necessarily focused on the consequences of our actions and our future as well as the future of others. Later, in Chapter 8, I will address this issue and its impact on females. We should be able to agree, men and women were created differently. However, and the differences should not prevent a lady from thinking like a man, as already coined by another well-known author.

The concept of accountability and responsibility has been prevalent throughout my life. It started with my upbringing at home and flourished as a result of my military career. I emphasize this because you will experience difficulty as a father trying to hold daughters or children accountable and responsible, particularly if you struggle with this issue yourself. As a father, it is so easy to talk the talk but can you walk the walk? Is this demonstrated in the way you currently handle your business? Daughters are always watching you, make no mistake about it.

Becoming a father before you are ready has a monumental impact, particularly in today's society. Juggling priorities, trying to manage your life as well as someone else's, providing health care, helping with doctor's visits, changing pampers, getting up in the middle of the night to feed and console, buying baby supplies, giving love and more time, making sacrifices, and finding steady employment are all part of the equation when you enter into fatherhood. Being responsible for another human being is serious stuff. As a man, whatever you do, do it right and do it to the best of your ability. What makes a man a man? Simply put, a man is someone who handles (all) his responsibilities.

We cannot choose our parents. We have zero influence on how our parents raised us. As growing children, we were busy focusing on enjoying life or possibly struggling to overcome everyday adversities. As children, it was not unusual for us to compare our upbringing with the upbringing of our friends. Many of us may have thought we were dealt a bad hand as we grew and began to try to figure life out. I believe no child is an accident. I believe whatever circumstances we are born into, is based on God's Master Plan. I am certain that whatever situation didn't kill you, will only strengthen you. I am confident that it is possible to take what is initially perceived as a negative environment or situation and profit from such perceived and unfortunate circumstances. I believe this because over and over again, I have seen others overcome these perceived negative situations and grow into very powerful and impactful individuals. Everybody has a story. Even though it may appear at times as if you and your situation are on an island all by yourselves; let me assure you that the island you think you are on is more populated than you will ever realize.

According to a report in *Fathers and Their Impact on Children's Well-Being*, even from birth, children who have an involved father are more likely to be emotionally secure, be confident to explore their surroundings, and, as they grow older, have better social connections. In summary, the modern day father can contribute to his children's health and well-being by maintaining a healthy relationship with the other parent even in cases of divorce or single parenting. Providing emotional and financial support, appropriate monitoring and discipline, and most importantly by establishing a permanent and loving presence in your children's' lives can also contribute to their overall health and well-being.

As I reflect, it occurred to me that my mother was not able to provide everything I desired. As an example, she was not able to provide financial support or guidance for college. She simply did not have the resources. But what she was lacking in this area, she was able to compensate for in other areas. She provided those things that were essential to my development as a man. She provided support, love, a home, and a deep appreciation for faith. Like me, during your developmental years, you may not have been provided with everything you thought you needed or desired. My take-a-way is as a parent you work with what you have. Use your resources wisely. As a parent, you sacrifice, show love, instill discipline, and model the things you want your children to emulate.

As you encounter fatherhood, life and parenting are about decision-making. Wise choices will ultimately determine the path you will take in life and in parenting. Even if your adolescent years were full of challenges above and beyond your control, there will be major crossroads along the way that will afford you the opportunity to change course.

"Children are gifts. They are not ours for the breaking. They are ours for the making."
— Dan Pearce —

"Children have never been very good at listening to their elders, but they have never failed to imitate them."
- James Baldwin –

Things to Build On:

- I was able to take a negative situation and turn it into a positive. Rather than use my reality as a crutch, I decided early in life to use this as a motivator.
- There are benefits of having to start life from the so called bottom; benefits of having to scratch and claw your way to rise above hardships. When life demands you re-visit adversity, you don't become unglued; overcoming adversity becomes instinctual or ingrained into your personal problem-solving thought process.
- Do not allow your issues to be passed on to the next generation.
- What makes a man a man? Simply put, a man is someone who handles (all) of his responsibilities.
- As a parent, you sacrifice, show love, instill discipline, and model the things you want your children to emulate.

Chapter 3 – The Impact of Marriage and Relationships on Co-Parenting, Single Parenting, and Blended Families

> *It's a great idea to privately play tag team with your spouse or co-parent. Sharing hard earned information can be vital to proactively solving the many challenges your daughter may face.*

Parents today are raising their children against a backdrop of increasingly diverse and for many, constantly evolving family forms. The declining number of children living in what is often deemed a "traditional" family has been largely supplanted by a rising number of children living with single or cohabiting parents.

Even though I am truly blessed to be in a traditional marriage, I recognize the fact that the world does not necessarily and fully operate that way any longer. The divorce rate is at an all-time high. Men and women are waiting much longer to consider marriage; for some, remaining single is a life style choice. Mothers and fathers are now co-parenting. Having children out of wedlock is very common. Contract co-parenting has even arrived on the scene and is slowly creeping into mainstream society. There are parents who have opted for alternative life-styles. There are blended families; yours plus mine equal ours. A large percentage of children are being raised by parents who are cohabiting but are not married. It doesn't really matter where you fit in this paradigm, the bottom line is you are taking your life's experiences, values, beliefs, and your DNA into becoming a father.

I have heard so many people say, parenting is the hardest thing they have ever done. I'm standing in agreement with this assertion. So, if true, and if or when you venture into fatherhood, why not equip yourself if you are not already a father or why not enhance your parenting skills if you are currently a father? How do you enhance your fathering skills? You enhance your skills by connecting with other fathers. You can confide and consult with someone who has already been where you are going. Also, observing, reading, and seeking support from reputable family, friends, or a professional counselor is beneficial. Most importantly, educate yourself, acknowledge what you don't know and share what you do know.

If you are co-parenting, I strongly urge you not to speak negatively about your daughter's mother when your daughter is spending time with you. If you openly speak negativity, this is actually harmful, extremely painful, and confusing. This is the time for adults to be adults. Please do not draw a child into an adult situation. Try to always be a positive influence rather than a negative influence. When co-parenting, if one parent or the other is not handling their business, this will ultimately be revealed as the daughter matures and grows older. Do not try and manipulate the relationship by revealing things that your daughter may not be mature enough to handle. When working towards solutions, do not attempt to match every perceived low blow with another low blow. As our former First Lady, Michelle Obama so eloquently and famously stated, "When they go low, you go high". Your daughter had zero input into why her mother and you cannot get along.

If you are dating, please be careful not to expose your daughter to too many different companions. In this situation, try being empathetic to what your daughter may be thinking or feeling about seeing you with multiple companions.

If you are seriously dating or engaged, ask yourself this question, do I want my daughter to be like the woman I'm dating or proposing marriage to? Please note, a woman can ask the same question about the man who is proposing. Ideally, the answer should be yes. You may be shocked to find out how men and women respond to this question. A father should be a role model for his daughter; an example of the husband she hopes to marry one day. A mother should be a role model for her daughter; modelling the type of woman she should grow up to be. Usually when I raise this question to others, the responses are varied and intriguing. This is one of the reasons why parenting is so vital. She may be fine and cute, but what kind of motherly influence will she have over your daughter? He may be "off the chain" physically but what kind of father figure will he be to his daughter? Not only that, the traditional wedding vows say, until death do us part, what do you do when the six pack (abs) turn into a spare tire? What do you do when the hour glass figure turns into something other than an hour glass? Can you still love and continue to parent without becoming selfish?

Fast forward to today. Baby momma drama or dead-beat dads have become so prevalent in our society. This situation can be a challenge for some co-parents. Your daughter (or son) can be successful coming out of a baby momma drama or dead-beat dad situation however, as a father (or mother), you will definitely have to work harder at doing whatever it is that you do (loving, providing, sharing, decision-making, communicating, role-modeling and etc.). During co-parenting, adults who deal with a non-ideal parenting situation oftentimes forget how their actions can impact their daughter(s) or son(s). I cannot even begin to imagine what life must be like in this situation from the child's perspective. At the end of the day, the primary concern for parents should be what is in the best interest of the child. Because of pride, egos, anger, pain, selfishness, and immaturity, parents oftentimes forget or ignore the fact that it's not about them, it's about the child you co-produced to bring into this world. So try hard to be the better person and try to keep harmony and peace for the sake of your child(ren).

Single parenting. I personally know so many single mothers who are raising children without the full support of the father. Please note, full support entails more than financial support. I do believe that overwhelmingly, as indicated in Chapter 4, the statistics support this claim. Conversely, I know there are single fathers who are also raising children without the full support of a mother. The difference is the statistics are not as staggering for single parent fathers. Even though I am a product of a single parent environment, I would be the first to admit that single parenting is even more challenging than dual-parenting. I believe strongly that many of the problems we encounter in society today with our youth and young adults are a direct reflection of absentee and dis-engaged fathers. So many of our children have no one to teach, guide, care for, or love them. This is not to take away from the accomplishments and struggles of parents from prior generations but I don't think too many would argue against the fact that the world we live in today is very different. Trying to balance work, life, and parenting duties and responsibilities is hard. This is where that village and support group comes into play; you cannot do it alone. That village or support group can be comprised of brothers, sisters, aunts, uncles, grandmothers, grandfathers, God Mothers, God Fathers, cousins, and dependable friends. The village or support group is enhanced when or if you work for an organization or Manager who is supportive of family values. No matter how hard, you push forward; you push forward because it's not about you; it's all about the well-being and the welfare of the daughter you helped bring into this world. Parenting is about sacrifice. To say it another way, making a sacrifice for the sake of your daughter is at the very core of being a father.

As engaged fathers, we all want our daughters to grow up to be successful. We may want to send them to the best schools and pay close attention to make sure they're completing their homework, and we sign them up for lots of extracurricular activities. We try to limit or at least monitor how much they talk on their phones or how much time they spend watching TV or playing video games. We encourage them to eat healthy and exercise. We make sure they feel loved and protected, and we encourage them to dream big and believe in themselves.

After doing all of this, there is still one critical thing you can do to help your daughter grow up to have a happy and successful life; that is being a model of what you want her to grow and develop into. One of the most important things a parent can do, although it's not the only thing we should do, is to model the behavior you want from your daughter. Show your daughter you care about her and she will purposefully try to emulate the way you are.

Are you mentally mature to become a parent? Are you spiritually mature to be a parent? Are you financially secure? Are you established in your career? Have you experienced or achieved all of those things in life that you wanted to experience and achieve prior to becoming a parent? Once you become a parent, it's not about you anymore; I fully understand that it is not uncommon to want your cake and ice cream too. Parenting, in and of itself is complicated. The decision to become a parent is one of the most daunting challenges life has to offer. It's really true, becoming a parent changes your life forever and is a lifelong endeavor.

Whether co-parenting, single parenting, or blended families, there is potential danger to not holding children accountable for their own actions and decisions. We have become a society where it has become so easy to place the blame or point the finger at someone else. Ownership of your actions and responsibilities is so important. For many reasons, children must be taught to do things they may not necessarily want to do. Understanding the impact of good decision-making, prioritizing, overcoming challenges and adversity can be essential to their overall growth.

I have personally spoken with numerous young females who acknowledge having a void in their lives as a result of a non-ideal relationship with their fathers. I am convinced that we (men) need to do everything within our power to right past wrongs. How do we begin to do this? Parents need to model the right behavior, show their daughters they love them, make them feel secure, provide support, and set their daughters up for challenges; letting them experience the consequences--good and bad--of their actions. Do this, and you'll have done what you can do to set your children on the path to success.

Parenting requires having to make some tough, demanding decisions. In my first book, *How To Enhance Your Professional Performance and Productivity*, I talked about the six major crossroads of life, #5 on that list was starting a family (including planning, raising, providing, educating, and role-modeling) for your children. The message is and ideally, there are four major crossroads of life you should prepare for prior to having children. If prior decisions in life or the cards you are dealt does not hold true to this ideal path, it does not mean that you cannot overcome your situation but what it means is that you will definitely encounter some additional challenges along the way.

The six major crossroads of life are:

1. Making a decision about your faith
2. Making an educational decision about your future (college, acquiring a trade, gaining a certification, or entering the military)
3. Finding stable employment/starting your career
4. Marriage
5. Starting a family (raising, providing, educating, and role modeling)
6. Transitioning into the golden years of life (leaving a legacy, giving back, and helping others)

"My father gave me the greatest gift anyone could give another person, he believed in me".

—Jim Valvano—

Things to Build On:

- Most importantly, educate yourself, acknowledge what you do not know and share what you do know.
- Try to always be a positive influence rather than a negative influence.
- A father should be a role model for his daughter; an example of the husband she hopes to marry one day.
- I believe strongly that many of the problems we encounter in society today with our youth and young adults are a direct reflection of absentee and dis-engaged fathers.
- Making a sacrifice for the sake of your daughter is at the very core of being a father.
- One of the most important things a parent can do, although it's not the only thing we should do, is to model the behavior you want from your daughter.

Chapter 4 – Statistics: What Do They Reveal? Why Are They Important? Why Should We Care?

> *If you fail to properly raise your children, in all likelihood you will end up playing a prominent role in raising your children's children.*
>
> Fanetta Dickens

Everyone is not a fan of data and statistics. In fact, reading through and trying to decipher data and statistics can be outright boring sometimes. There is, however, a place for data and statistics when attempting to determine and understand solutions to complex problems and issues. Parenting and raising children in today's society can be placed into the category of complex issues. Considering the many challenges facing parents and their children, I wanted to take a moment to explore some of the disadvantages and everyday challenges that many of us face. Many of the disadvantages and challenges can only be understood through the concept of data and statistics. While acknowledging this maybe somewhat of an unorthodox approach, I believe that some of the information contained in data and statistics is substantial enough to share. Truthfully, I am speaking of the type of information that many of us may not necessarily pursue on our own; oftentimes, we perish because of a lack of knowledge. Based on data and statistics, it's important for us to understand how the results can impact society in general, parenting, and the challenges we face on a daily basis as we strive to ensure our family's well-being.

Being a parent is hard. Parenting was not easy for our forefathers and there is no easy sailing in sight for us and our immediate future. I assure you that if your parents made it appear that what they were doing was easy, it is because there were some serious hard work and sacrifices going on behind the scene. Through data and statistics, I want to take a little time to examine this notion that parenting and particularly fatherhood is hard. Every household is different. Every parent (father) is different. Every child is different. As Baby Boomers and Generation X'ers, the world is certainly different from the world we inherited from our parents and the world will most certainly be different when our children inherit their rightful places from us. When you consider the impact on parents in general and fathers specifically, the challenges of today should make you think long and hard prior to making the decision to become a father.

Several facts that cannot be overlooked are the social, economic, educational, employment, criminal justice, and housing disadvantages suffered by people of color and how these disadvantages can alter and impact the parenting process or the journey. Because I am an African American father, it would be prudent for me to express the additional challenges of fatherhood as I strive to lead, protect, provide, and offer security for my family. To reinforce my position on the realities of African Americans confronting additional challenges, I decided to share some data that reinforces the struggle encountered by African Americans. The purpose of providing this data and statistics is not to examine the "why"; the purpose is to inform and to ignite a perspective of "what will you do to change this" and "how does this data impact your ability to rear your children"? The acknowledgement of expressing myself from an African American male's perspective is not meant to discourage, diminish, or discount other ethnic groups from benefiting from this publication.

Criticism of Systemic Racism

Critics of the juvenile justice system believe that the system is unfairly stacked against minority youth. Minority youth are disproportionately represented in incarcerated populations relative to their representation in the general population. A recent report from the *National Council on Crime and Delinquency* found that minority youth are treated more severely than white youth at every point of contact with the system—from arrest, to detention, to adjudication, to incarceration—even when charged with the same crime. In 1995, African American youths made up 12% of the population, but were arrested at rates double those for Caucasian youths. The trend towards adult adjudication has had implications for the racial make-up of the juvenile prison population as well. Minority youth who are tried in adult courts are much more likely to be sentenced to serve prison time than white youth offenders arrested for similar crimes.

Profiles of Youth in Custody

A report by the Federal Office of Juvenile Justice and Delinquency Prevention and U.S. Department of Justice, "Survey of Youth in Residential Placement: Youth's Needs and Services," used data gathered during interviews from more than 7,000 youths who are in custody. The report's findings include: 70% of youth in custody reported that they had "had something very bad or terrifying" happen to them in their lives. 67% reported having seen someone severely injured or killed; 26% of those surveyed said they felt as if "life was not worth living," and 22% reported having tried to commit suicide at some point in their lives; 84% of the youth surveyed said they had used marijuana, compared to a rate of 30% among their peers in the general population; 30% reported having used crack or cocaine, compared with only 6% in the general population. The report noted a significant gap between the profiles of boys and girls, with girls often reporting more pronounced difficulties: 63% of girls reported having problems with anger, whereas 47% of boys did; 49% of girls reported having hallucinatory experiences, whereas only 16% of boys did; 37% of girls reported having suicidal thoughts and feelings, whereas only 18% of boys did. Facilities that treat such youth also were shown to be inadequate in some core areas, according to the Justice Department. Among youth who reported four or more recent substance related problems, only about 60% said they had been provided with substance abuse counseling in their current facility. Many youth in custody reported having attention problems and difficulties in school. Once in custody, only 45% report spending 6 hours a day or more in school, meaning that their learning time is below that of the general population.

Violence in School

Violence has become a reality at the majority of public schools in America. More than 73% of all public schools in the United States have recorded at least one incident of violent crime during the 2009-2010 school year. These type of crimes include fights, robbery, physical attacks or threats to do so with or without weapons, and sexually related offenses. When only looking at middle and high schools that number increases from 73% to more than 90%.
When broken down into racial/ethnic categories, 82% of schools that are more than 50% Black have recorded at least one violent crime compared to 77% of majority Hispanic schools and 71% of majority White schools.

Although fewer Black schools recorded between 6 and 9 incidents of violent crime than White and Hispanic schools that changed when comparing schools who have more than 20 recorded incidents of violent crime. In such cases where violent incidents were more frequent 29% of majority Black schools recorded 20 or more incidents compared to 22% of Hispanic and 16% of white schools.

Gangs in School

Data reveals Hispanics are more active in school gangs than any other large racial or ethnic group. Gangs, whether or not they are involved in violent or illegal activity, are visible by about one third of Black students' ages 12 to 16 in American schools. Whites in the same age group reported 50% less gang presence than African Americans. Urban areas are usually looked upon as the face of gang activity in the United States. However, 60% of Black students reported no gang presence at school which includes the school building, on school property, on a school bus, or going to and from school.

The biggest surprise might be that 35% of Black rural students reported gangs in their schools in 2009. This is a large increase from 22.5% in 2001, while during the same time period reported gang presence in suburban schools by African Americans decreased from 25% to 20%.

Overall, reported gang presence among all students ages 12 to 18, regardless of race or location, remained the same at 20% from 2001 to 2009. Also, 9th and 10 graders reported higher gang presence than all other grades including 11th and 12th graders by a few percentage points over the same 8 year period.

Poverty in Black America

According to the 2014 U.S. Census Bureau ACS study, 27% of all African American men, women and children live below the poverty level compared to just 11% of all Americans. An even higher percentage (38%) of Black children live in poverty compared to 22% of all children in America. The poverty rate for working-age Black women (26%) which consists of women ages 18 to 64 is higher than that of working-age Black men (21%).

Poverty rates for Black families vary based on the family type. While 23% of all Black families live below the poverty level only 8% of Black married couple families live in poverty which is considerably lower than the 37% of Black families headed by single women who live below the poverty line. The highest poverty rates (46%) are for Black families with children which are headed by single Black women. This is significant considering more than half (55%) of all Black families with children are headed by single women.

African American males ages 16 to 64 had a lower participation rate in the labor force (67%) compared to 'all males' (80%) (See below table). Labor force participation refers to the percent of men who were either working or looking for work. Males not in the labor force include those who may be full time students, disabled, and others who are not looking or gave up looking for employment for other reasons.

EARNINGS AND EMPLOYMENT

Age 16 to 64	Black Men	All Men
Percent who are in the labor force	67%	80%
Percent who are unemployed	11.2%	7.3%
Below poverty level	26%	15%
Ages 16 and up		
Median earnings for 2013	$37,290	$48,099
Worked full-time, year-round	37%	48%
Earnings NOT from full-time work	23%	23%
No earnings all year	40%	30%

Occupation Type

White collar	42%	75%
Blue collar	36%	17%
Service occupation	23%	8%

The 37% of African American males who worked full time all year in 2013 had median earnings of $37,290 in 2013 compared to $48,099 for 'all men' (above table). Of Black males' ages 16 to 64 years old, 40% had no earnings in 2013 which was higher than the 30% with no earnings of 'all men' in the same age group. Also a larger percentage of Black males 16 to 64 were unemployed than for 'all men' (11.2% compared to 7.3%) and were living below the poverty level (26%) than 'all men' (15%).

Compared to 'all men' in the United States Black men who worked were much less likely to work in occupations that may be considered white collar and were much more likely to hold blue collar or service jobs. Only 42% of working Black men held white collar jobs compared to 75% of 'all men'. For the purpose of the Earning and Employment table above, white collar occupations include but are not limited to jobs in management, business, computers, office, legal, education, etc.

African American Income

**Black Median Household income: $35,481
(all races $53,657)
All Black Workers 2015 weekly earnings: $624
(all races $803)
Black Men weekly earnings: $652
(All men $889)
Black Women weekly earnings: $608
(All women $721)**

SOURCE: 2015 3rd Quarter: Bureau of Labor Statistics – 16 Years or Older & 2014 Census Bureau, American Community Survey

During the 1990s, African American income grew tremendously. By 2000, 56% of African American households had an annual income of $35K or more compared to just 36% in 1969. However, due to the recession, that number dropped to just 51% by 2014 reversing much of these gains. The most dramatic change during the most recent recession was the percentage of Black households making under $15K (from 19% in 2000 to 24% in 2010) which was well below the poverty line for families.

Black Family Income

	Blacks	All USA
Families	**8,763,279**	76,509,262
Median family income (dollars)	**$40,946**	$62,527
Married-couple family	**43.9%**	72.9%
Median income (dollars)	**$65,914**	$76,035
Male household, no	**9.7%**	7.3%
Median income (dollars)	**$33,860**	42, .588
Female householder, no husband present	**46.3%**	19.8%
Median income (dollars)	**$25,594**	$30,486

Source: US Census Bureau 2012 American Community Survey
BlackDemographics.com

Although incomes for African Americans have improved significantly since the Civil Rights era, they are still lower than the national average. For example, the median income for Black families is $20 thousand a year less than the national median income.

Incarceration

According to the US Department of Justice, more African Americans have sentences for drug convictions (of more than one year) in state prisons than any other offense. Approximately 122,600 Blacks were under state jurisdiction for drugs accounting for 21.1% of all Black state inmates in December 2009. This is higher than the 17.8% of all inmates incarcerated for drug offenses. Robbery was the cause for the second largest percentage of Black inmates with 18.9%, followed by property crimes which include burglary, larceny, motor vehicle theft, and others at 15.2%. Murder convictions were responsible for 14.4% of African Americans in state prisons.

According to the U.S. Department of Education, 1,034,000 African American men were enrolled in a degree granting institution in 2009 compared to 841,000 who were counted in the nation's jails and prisons during the same year. And of those Black men in jail and prison, only 164,400 are of typical college age (18-24). In fact, even a decade ago when overall numbers suggested there were more black men in jail than in school, college aged Black men enrolled in a degree granting institution, which far outnumbered their peers who were incarcerated. Source: U.S. Department of Education, National Center for Education Statistics and U.S. Department of Justice Programs Bureau of Justice Statistics.

Education

In 2013 about 48% of Black men 25 and older attended college although half of them did not complete a degree compared to 58% of 'all men' who attended college.

Education

In 2013 about 48% of Black men 25 and older attended college although half of them did not complete a degree compared to 58% of 'all men' who attended college.

EDUCATIONAL ATTAINMENT (25 & UP)

	Black Men	All Men
Less than high school diploma	**18%**	14%
High school graduate or GED)	**35%**	28%
Some college, no degree	**24%**	21%
Associates degree	**7%**	7%
Bachelor's degree	**17%**	30%
Attended College	**48%**	58%

The biggest disparity between Black men and 'all men' in America is with those who have a bachelor's degree. Only 17% of Black men have a bachelor's degree compared to 30% of 'all men'. Second is the number of Black men who finished high school but did not pursue higher education, 35% compared to 28% of 'all men'.

The percentage of Black men who have an associate's degree (7%) is equal to that of 'all men' (7%) in America. Only 18% of Black men over 25 did not complete high school. This is still higher than the percent for men of all races and ethnic groups together. Source: U.S. Department of Education.

Employment

Although African Americans have an unemployment rate almost double that of the overall population, the Black workforce is just as diverse. Since the federal government was one of the first to integrate, African Americans have been over represented in that sector. More than 20% of the Black working population over 16 years old are employees of the federal, state, or local government which is just over 5 percentage points higher than the national average. On the other end, a much smaller percentage of African Americans are self-employed (3.6%) than the national average of 6.2%.

Marriage

Marriage has been a declining institution among all Americans and this decline is even more evident in the Black community. In 2014 only 29% of African Americans were married compared to 48% of all Americans. 50% of African Americans have never been married compared to 33% of all Americans.

In 2012 *The U.S Census Bureau* released a report that studied the history of marriage in the United States. They discovered some startling statistics when calculating marriage by race. They found that African Americans age 35 and older were more likely to be married than White Americans from 1890 until sometime around the 1960s. Not only did they swap places during the 60s but in 1980 the number of NEVER married African Americans began a staggering climb from about 10% to more than 25% by 2010 while the percentage for White women remained under 10% and just over 10% for White men. Source: U.S. Census Bureau, 2014 American Community Survey 1-Year Estimates.

According to the 2013 U.S. Census Bureau, the African American male population is 21.5 million. The "all other" male population is 97.9 million.

With regard to what is revealed in the above-mentioned data and statistics, perhaps many of us, all ethnicities, have become somewhat immune or grown callous to the impact of this information. Rather than ignoring or feeding into further escalation of the root causes and contribution to this phenomenon, each one of us should ask ourselves, what is it that I can do to turn this negativity around? What actions can I take? How can I make a difference? The answers are concealed in a call to action. This includes teaching your children, attending Parent Teacher Conferences, establishing a rapport with your child's teacher, taking responsibility for our actions as well as the actions of our children, participating in the community, and volunteering.

You can also take a strong interest in political and community affairs. What do I mean? Do you vote in all elections? Juvenile and county judgeships are important, particularly if, God forbid, your child has to encounter the system. Local school boards are critical. Who on the school board represents your interest? Civic associations impact your immediate community, what does your neighborhood's quality of life programs look like? Funding for libraries and local children's programs will slowly deteriorate if no one takes an interest.

What kind of relationship does the local community have with local law enforcement? Ever heard of the Citizen's Police Academy? Do you know who your neighbors are? The point here is for the sake and future of your children. It is beneficial for you, the parent, to get involved. You can invest in and become more protective of your most prized earthly possession: your child.

I can say confidently, the impact for change starts at home. If we accept the notion that leadership, support, and protection starts at home with fathers, then the impetus is squarely on our shoulders. Whatever we see as our role, fathers should have sharpened tools in their personal toolboxes, ready to help make a difference. Once reviewed and if you accept this data and statistics as impactful, then clearly, every phase of our lives and the lives of our children are at risk. Speak positively into the life of your daughter. If she doesn't hear positivity at home she won't know how to share positivity into the lives of others. Love, forgiveness, appreciation, and affection are the attributes I am referring to. Children will usually mimic what they see and hear.

One could conclude that there are definitive challenges facing people of color as we try to achieve our piece of the American dream of caring and providing for our families.
Self-liberation begins with information, education, an open dialogue-conversation, and a willingness to do something.

"Without data, you are just another person with an opinion".

W. Edwards Deming

"I cannot think of any need in childhood as strong as the need for a father's protection".

—Sigmund Freud—
"When my father didn't have my hand…he had my back".

—Linda Poindexter—

Things to Build On:

- I assure you that if your parents made it appear that what they were doing was easy, it is because there were some serious hard work and sacrifices going on behind the scene.
- Minority youth are disproportionately represented in incarcerated populations relative to their representation in the general population.
- The impact for change starts at home.
- Children will usually mimic what they see and hear.
- Self-liberation begins with information, education, an open dialogue-conversation, and a willingness to do something.

Chapter 5 – The Two Basic Needs – Love and Security

> *You can never overstate to your daughter just how much you love her; by doing so she will not clamor to hear this from someone else, outside of the home environment*

Ideally, you should be your daughter's first male love! This is so critical. Going forward, your love or lack of love will go a long way in developing her true grasp of love in future relationships.

I believe love and security are the two most basic needs for our children. I believe this, not because of some scientific research but because of my 27 years of on the job training as a father. In Ephesians 5:25 (NKJV), the Bible admonishes men, "Husbands, love your wives, as Christ loved the church and gave himself up for her". In 1 Peter 3:7 (NKJV), we are reminded, "Likewise, husbands, live with your wives in an understanding way, showing honor to the woman as the weaker vessel, since they are heirs with you of the grace of life, so that your prayers may not be hindered". Reference to the weaker vessel implies a desire to feel and be loved.

Here me out on this, our wives and daughters are females and hopefully, one day our daughters will become wives and mothers. If men are to love their wives, be understanding, and be honorable, isn't it an expectation or a continuation to do the same with your daughters? As a father, you demonstrate love, fulfilling the need of the weaker vessel. Essentially, you are modeling for your daughter what she should see and expect once she becomes a woman, wife, or mother.

For some of us, love can be complicated. Love requires us to care for someone to a greater extent than ourselves. Love demands expression, emotions, honesty, trust, and sometimes true transparency. If we are honest with ourselves as men, we sometimes struggle with these issues. I would suggest to you that some men may fear love and commitment. Oftentimes, we are more comfortable demonstrating rather than voicing our love. Then again, some men may feel intimidated, threatened, or even vulnerable by the idea of expressing love. I might also add, many of us (just like women) may have experienced rejection or hurt from a previous relationship which may factor into our ability or inability to open our hearts fully to someone else.

Let's see if we can drill down a little deeper so that we can gain a greater understanding. As men, we would experience tremendous growth and prosperity in love if we can learn to:

- Love God; spiritual connection
- Understand that one of the greatest displays of love here on earth is the love that a mother displays for her child. The bond between mother and child may be difficult for some men to grasp. It's called unconditional love.
- Open our hearts and minds to understand a mother's love, our wives' (if married) care and commitment, and our daughter's needs and vulnerabilities; they can help teach us more about love than we ever imagined.

There has been ongoing debates about the different types of love. Some psychologist and supporters of the ancient Greeks would argue there are three, four, six, seven, or maybe even eight types of love. To the best of my knowledge, there is one source that is unquestionable. That one source is the Holy Bible. The bible speaks specifically about three types of love; Eros, philia, and agape and implies another, storge. Let's examine the following:

1. Agape: Unconditional Love

Agape speaks of the most powerful, noblest type of love: sacrificial love. *Agape* love is more than a feeling—it is an act of will. Agape is the term that defines God's immeasurable, incomparable love for humankind. It is his ongoing, outgoing, self-sacrificing concern for lost and fallen people. Agape extends beyond emotions. It's much more than a feeling or sentiment. Agape love is active. It demonstrates love through actions.

2. Phileo: Brotherly Love

Philia refers to brotherly love and is most often exhibited in a close friendship. Best friends will display this generous and affectionate love for each other as each seeks to make the other happy. Since *phileo* love involves feelings of warmth and affection toward another person, we do not show phileo love toward our enemies.

3. Eros: Erotic Love

Eros is passionate or sexual love (*Eros* is the source of the English word *erotic*). While *Eros* is important within a marriage relationship and is created by God (see Song of Solomon in the Bible), it can also be abused or mistaken for *storge* love. Within the boundary of marriage, Eros is to be celebrated.

4. Storge: Love towards Family

Storge is an affectionate love, the type of love one might have for family. It is a naturally occurring, unforced type of love. Storge is family love, the bond among mothers, fathers, sons, daughters, sisters, and brothers. Storge is further defined as cherishing one's kindred, especially parents and children.

As men and fathers, we have a desire to be respected. The females in our lives have a desire to be loved.

Parents are the first two people who get the opportunity to teach children what love looks like, and our children are counting on us to prove that love is real. Children want to see their imperfect, dysfunctional parents dance in front of them, say "I love you" when they get off the phone, pray together, kiss as they say goodbye and speak highly of each other. These moments of affection provide assurance to our children that the world isn't all bad. Things are going to be OK at home.

Demonstrating marital love to our children is a privilege, a unique opportunity to be both a good parent and a good spouse. To love each other well is to love our children well.

According to the American Psychological Association, research on the role of fathers suggests that the influence of fatherly love on children's development is as great as the influence of a mother's love. Fatherly love helps children develop a sense of their place in the world, which helps their social, emotional and cognitive development and functioning. Moreover, children who receive more love from their fathers are less likely to struggle with behavioral or substance abuse problems.

Security – Emotional, Physical, and Financial Support

If you are not ready to make sacrifices for others, then you probably should think twice before having children. If you are already a father, you may want to reconsider how you view the needs of others over your needs. There are personal and professional sacrifices that must be made on behalf of your children. I'll share one example of a professional sacrifice. I have always loved sports. When my oldest daughter was around three or four years old, I was an up and coming high school and small college basketball referee. I had risen to the highly sought after position of Assignment Secretary and clinician; scheduling, training and certifying other referees. At that time, some colleagues even thought I may have exhibited the necessary skills to referee at the highest level. I might add, the extra pay didn't hurt either. As my wife was working the evening shift, I sometimes found myself picking up our daughter from one child care facility and immediately taking her to another baby sitter so I could travel to my games; forcing my wife to finally pick up our daughter after 10 pm. Once I saw the puzzled look on my daughter's face after a few of these episodes, a little voice on the inside of me began screaming, this is not right! Shortly thereafter, I walked away, never to return to officiating basketball again. I have no regrets because in my heart, I knew this was the right thing to do. Though a bit old school, I'll also share one example of a personal sacrifice. My late mother raised four children without their father. She decided to remain a widow for 17 years because she could not trust another man with the responsibility of having authority over her children. While growing up, I cannot recall my mother having a man spend a night at our home. I am not saying she did not have a male friend, I am saying, I do not recall anyone coming near her bedroom while her children were at home. My mother always said, when her youngest child left home, she would re-marry; once I left home, she stayed true to her word and finally remarried.

From a very young age, there was a process I tried to instill in my daughters. That process was go to school, complete your education, start your career, and then consider a serious relationship or marriage, in that order. In conversation, every time I took advantage of the opportunity to drive home my point, my daughters would respond with a slightly sarcastic and loving response of, "Yes we know Dad". If you were to dig down a little deeper in this process, the implication or the subtle, unspoken statement is "no babies until you have fulfilled your stated goals". This was the way I attacked this issue but admittedly, my wife also hit them from the flanks. In other words, getting this point across was like warfare. Lives were at stake! Let me also say this, a daughter's dreams and goals can still be fulfilled if she were to become pregnant before marriage if there is a support system in place. However, expect the challenges to increase if that is the case. At the end of the day, communication, staying focused, smart decision-making, and self-discipline are keys to open discussions about unplanned pregnancies. Remind your daughter that there is a danger when you think that this can only happen to other people and cannot happen to me.

Let me share a few general thoughts impacting security:

- It's important that you spend one-on-one time with your daughter; if she is receptive, this shared time is beneficial for her as well as for you. Subtlety pick her brains about what is currently going on in her life as well as gain insight on her future plans and ideas.
- Transparency. I often revealed to my daughters how they were much better teenagers and young adults than I ever was; I talked about my faults and shortcomings
- Borrowed principles; my Pastor revealed that he personally delivered roses at school to his daughter on Valentine's Day. Imagine how she must have felt. One celebrity deducted a $1 weekly payment from her son's allowance to teach him about contributing to the needs of the household. A former employee shared with me how her father taught her about keeping up with and performing some minor, required maintenance on her car. The point here is as Dads, we do not know everything. Therefore when we occasionally encounter an idea or successful parenting technique, don't hesitate to borrow it.

- As a father, you are competing with society & social media. A large percentage of young men, particularly African Americans grow up in households without male role models. The use of the B-word and the N-word is rampart is today's society. Sexting is ok. Self-indulgence, self-promotion, and self-gratification are wide-spread. Advertisements and marketing does not always project young females in a positive light.
- Every time my daughters entered or left our home, greeting one another with a kiss was expected
- I told my daughters that I would become their friend when they were a.) Out of my house and b.) financially independent
- While teaching them about decision-making, I often facilitated (guided) them into considering all options; testing them into selecting the best course of action. Finally, I would offer my agreement/disagreement about the topic.
- If you fail to properly raise your children, in all likelihood you will end up playing a prominent role in raising your grandchildren
- When my daughters were out at night, it was difficult for me to fall into a deep sleep until I knew they were safely in the house
- Once they were given cars, I was responsible for monitoring vehicle maintenance; oftentimes I would inconspicuously inspect their vehicles while parked in the driveway.
- They didn't need to, but both of my daughters acquired jobs while in high school. You can gain life and social skills from a part-time job. Some of the lessons include responsibility, team work, decision making, establishing relationships, dealing with authority figures (bosses), the importance of engaging and interacting with others and understanding diversity.

- Daughters must learn that every disagreement with a man does not have to turn into an all-out war. Learning to disagree, particularly with someone of the opposite sex is an art. This understanding could be useful in relationships as well as on the job. Where possible, learn to become strategic. Be opportunistic; live to fight another day, perhaps another way.
- Engaging my daughter's friends; encouraging their participation in family events and celebrations were important to me. This provided me with the opportunity to get to know who my daughters were hanging out with.
- Children are not self-sufficient. They must rely on their parents to provide the essentials of life: love, food, clothing, shelter, security, growth, and guidance.
- Being a father and providing advice does not cease when your children leave your house. Parenting is a life-long endeavor. Please keep in mind however, to allow for an appropriate invitation before you proceed to offer advice to your children once they become self-sufficient, responsible, and independent adults.

Let's talk about sex. While writing this book, I struggled with identifying the appropriate chapter to talk about sex. Should I talk about it in this chapter, Chapter 5, "The Two Basic Needs – Love and Security" or should I have addressed this issue in Chapter 8, "Transformation from Girls to Women and Advice about Boys/Men"? I chose to talk about sex in this chapter because the old school side of me prevailed. That is sex is connected to love, which further implies marriage. For the most part, my wife took the lead on this topic. But who do you turn to if you are a single parent raising a daughter? Even if you are not married, your daughter still needs to have this discussion with her father because the male perspective is crucial to her development. This discussion is not easy by any stretch of the imagination. You start out by making your daughter feel comfortable about being open long before you reach this topic. When they come to you with intimate and tough topics, don't trip; you are setting the foundation for future communication. When this happened to me, it took every fiber in my body to maintain my poker face; no excitement, no disappointment, and no shock and awe. The real question is, how do you know when it's time to have this discussion? The answer is, it depends. It depends on what? It depends on the maturity level of your daughter, her activities, level of inquisitiveness, growth, conversation, and her physical development. Every child is different and every parent is different. What you say depends on your spiritual beliefs, morals, principles, and core values. It doesn't matter what your position may be, the potential consequences for having sex is a universal concern for all fathers. The bottom line is you cannot afford not to have this conversation. There is no easy way out. If you fail to be the first male in her life to have this conversation, the reality is that another male may beat you to it.

Every sexual encounter is a potential parenting encounter. Every sexual partner is a potential father or mother. If you have a choice, a planned decision will initially produce a more positive life experience than an unplanned situation. Let me add, one of the biggest mistakes made by young women is to attempt to secure love from a man by having his baby. To be fair, abstinence from sex is an individual responsibility. However, protecting yourself from an unplanned pregnancy is a dual responsibility.

Bend but Don't Break Concept

I am a product of the Baby Boomers Generation. My daughters are Millennials. As a parent, you must find a balance between what is old school versus what is new school. As an example, some attributes are never outdated, i.e. self-discipline, responsibility, accountability, honesty & etc. However, technology, social media, and educational opportunities forces you to view life differently.

As previously stated, I love sports. There is an old adage in football that says, "Bend but don't break". What does this mean? In football, the offense's job is to move the ball downfield, either quickly or methodically (making first downs) so that ultimately, touch downs (six points) or fields goals (three points) can be scored. The defenses' role is to prevent the offense from scoring a touchdown or a field goal so that the team is placed in a position to ultimately win the game. When adhering to the "bend but don't break" concept, the defense will allow some advancement of the ball down the field until there is a threat by the offense to maneuver itself into scoring position. The closer the offense gets to the goal line or scoring position, the harder the defense plays and the more dug in the defense becomes. The defense will bend by allowing the offense some room to maneuver the ball downfield but it will not break by allowing the offense to score.

Perhaps as fathers parenting daughters, we need to adopt the "bend but don't break" concept. We probably wish we could just lock our daughters up and deny them all contact with the outside world but this is not possible. With respect to parenting, there are some old school concepts that we should hold on to while at the same time, we must begrudgingly give in to those things that we know are outdated. We shouldn't have to discuss what old school concepts we need to hold on to versus what new ideas we need to give in to; as you might imagine, the list is just too long. Plus, what works in one man's house may not necessarily work in another man's house. Ideally, we must find a balance between the old and the new when it comes to parenting. Once we find this middle ground, I equate this to the "bend but don't break" concept; concede a little but with limitations.

You don't want to give your daughter everything, you want her to earn and appreciate what she has or have achieved.

Okay, the million dollar question, once they become young adults, when will they leave to a place of their own? Today, statistics reveal that children are opting to stay with their parents much longer than at any time in history. Why? I'm not sure but I'll attempt to offer up some reasons:

- Finding a "real" job is hard. The economy is not as favorable as it once was. The cost of living is very expensive.
- With a median household income of $40,581, millennials earn 20 percent less than boomers did at the same stage of life, despite being better educated, according to a new analysis of Federal Reserve data by the advocacy group Young Invincibles.
- Parents are no longer in a rush to encourage their children to leave home
- If children just happened to be contributing towards maintaining the home, some parents are benefiting financially from this arrangement.
- Children are slow to develop what we will call "real life skills". I'm talking about, things like managing a budget, saving, prioritizing, setting SMART goals, and disciplining themselves to buy what you need versus buying what you desire. Note: SMART = Specific, Measurable, Attainable, Relevant, and Trackable/Timely.
- As parents, we went out of our way to ensure our children were afforded opportunities that were not afforded to us and as a result, we may have handicapped their growth.
- Lack of motivation; apathy
- Fear

When will your child leave home or how long will they stay? This very issue, in my view is the #1 issue when dealing with young adults. It is not unusual for a father to feel one way while a mother feels another. I have seen this issue divide households. How do you handle this situation? The answer again is, it depends. It depends on your values, beliefs, financial status, emotions, and so much more. There is no concrete answer; every household is different.

When my daughters initially left for college, my wife and I celebrated being "empty nesters". You could walk around the house in your underwear, you didn't have to lock the door to the master bedroom at night, didn't have to argue about who performed what chores, and didn't have to run around behind others turning out lights. Those were the good ole days. However, that did not last long; I call my daughters temporary return the "transitioning phase".

I would suggest establishing guidelines and boundaries for young adults who return home or are slow to leave. When my daughters returned home from college, my wife and I created a contract. Yes, an actual contract. See appendix #1 on page 121. When we initially sat down to discuss this contract in detail, the look on my daughter's faces was priceless. Later, we may not have held them to the letter of the law with regard to the contract but the subtle messages had been sent. This definitely gave them something to ponder. Periodically, whenever an unexpected debate or concern came up, I would refer back to the contract. After all, the parents are the homeowners. Fondly, I sometimes compare my approach to an adult child living at home versus the approach my dear mother had. I'll give you a small glimpse into how my mother approached teenagers living in her house. I can recall violating her curfew one time; she flat out refused to open the door. I had to spend the night outside in my car. There was no debate. My mother's action reverberated how serious she was about parenting. I wish I could share additional exchanges my mother and I had about situations where if you think you are grown but those exchanges maybe a bit too raw and uncut for me to reveal in this book. There would have been some definite "tough love" going on back in the day regarding staying in her house if you thought you were an adult. Still, the contractual exercise caused me to reflect and it was a wonderful lesson about real life. I enjoyed it.

As fathers, oftentimes the calculated seed you plant today, can yield tremendous results later.

"A father's tears and fears are unseen, his love is unexpressed, but his care and protection remains as a pillar of strength throughout our lives".

—Ama H. Vanniarachchy—

Things to Build On:

- I would submit to you that some men fear love and commitment.
- I might also add, many of us (just like women) may have experienced rejection or hurt from a previous relationship which may factor into our ability to not open our hearts fully to someone else.
- Parents are the first two people who get the opportunity to teach children what love looks like, and our children are counting on us to prove that love is real.
- Fatherly love help children develop a sense of their place in the world, which helps their social, emotional and cognitive development and functioning.
- Transparency; I often tell my daughters how they were much better teenagers and young adults than I ever was. I talked about my faults and shortcomings.
- It doesn't matter what your position may be, the potential consequence for having sex is a universal concern for all fathers. If you fail to be the first male in her life to have this conversation, the reality is that another male may beat you to it.
- To be fair, abstinence from sex is an individual responsibility, however, protecting yourself from an unplanned pregnancy is a dual responsibility.
- I would suggest establishing guidelines and boundaries for young adults who return home or are slow to leave.

Chapter 6– Building a Core Foundation in the Home and Through Family Bonding

> *A daughter's relationship with her father develops the core foundation for how she will interact with boys and ultimately men.*

The importance of a formal education can never be overstated. In today's society, education is a must for your children. We all are fully aware of the benefits of a quality education. I subscribe to parents doing everything within their power to promote well-roundedness. Aside from a formal, quality education, exposure to different cultures, people, places, and things broadens your child's perspective of life. This perspective begins by building a core foundation in the home and through family bonding.

Building a core foundation and family bonding starts early. When my eldest daughter was an infant, around two years old, I recall taking a four day, 1400 mile round-trip to my mother's house, alone, with my daughter. My mother in law, who may say she doesn't recall, was a little concerned about me taking this trip alone with my infant daughter. My wife had zero concerns about my abilities to go it alone. I was a first time dad; I was a little nervous but I had confidence that I could do it. I had a blast and I was so proud of myself for pulling it off.

I took great pride in being able to handle the needs of my infant daughters. This included feedings, pamper changes, and everything in between. My approach was when others think I can't do something, I take pride in proving them wrong. I am by nature a competitive person, so I viewed performing daddy duties as winning over those who didn't think I could handle such challenges. As a father, performing daddy duties is simply the right thing to do. Not only that, you will quickly discover that there will be times when mommy simply needs a break.

My family was very fortunate in exposing our daughters to numerous cultural, social, educational, natural, and sports related excursions. If you are unable to do this, there are still creative ways to take full advantage of the opportunity to offer your children various levels of exposure outside of the usual and formal educational apparatuses. The library does wonders for the adventurous mind. Local parks. Community centers. What about the zoo? Local plays and the theater. Museums. Theme parks. Regular visits to the local colleges or universities. How about a ride in the car to some nearby location away from your own neighborhood? What about exposure to different types of cuisines? Visits to historical places of interests. Lake or the beach? The list of potential opportunities go on and on.

There is one particular trip that stands out in my mind that my wife and I took our daughters on when they were about 10 and 13. The trip was to New Orleans. My wife and I debated whether or not we would allow our daughters to stroll down Bourbon Street. Well, we did! I can remember vividly my wife clutching one daughter by the hand while I was clutching the other. I can remember the wild-eyed look of astonishment in their eyes. After returning home, I do recall one of my daughters informing us that when she grows up she wanted to move to New Orleans. Now that she is a young adult, that did not happen. Perhaps many of you would be opposed to such exposure at a young age but here is my rationale. I would rather my daughters have certain exposures in my presence rather than outside of my presence. Also, I liked the fact that they were able to ask questions and we were able to answers their questions on the spot. Finally, another rationale was once my daughters became adults, they would not be overwhelmed or in awe of similar exposures that someone other than me may want to introduce them to. It's like, if a daughter constantly hears in her home that she is loved and beautiful, then it should not be a big deal when she hears it outside of the home because she's heard that before. She can respond by saying, "My daddy tells me that all the time". I might add, telling them is one thing, but showing or expressing your love is just as important.

One of my all-time great experiences was taking my two daughters and three nieces (yes that's five young girls), on a 2,000 mile round trip journey, in a minivan to Disney World. At that time, the girls were between the ages of seven to 16. We rode, I drove, and we sang and just had fun. Upon arrival, we dedicated one whole day to each theme park. Once we were inside the theme parks, I mostly delegated to the oldest and positioned myself at several nice and strategically located establishments to unwind and take it all in. We didn't have cell phones for everyone back then; we used walkie-talkies to communicate. We had a blast! As I reflect, I have no idea what made me take on this challenge. What I do know is, this experience had a positive impact on everyone, including me. Fast forward to today, my three nieces now have children of their own. They have tried to convince me to recreate that experience by doing the same thing with their children. After years of negotiations, I have not given in! This is an example of how family bonding can have a positive, life-time impact on young girls. Every now and then, at family gatherings, they'll pull out the videos to do a little reminiscing. I can also recall sitting down with my daughters watching television shows like "16 and Pregnant". They did not ask me to do this but they welcomed my participation. During and after the various episodes, we would talk about what was happening with the show's participants. These occasions turned out to be teachable moments; actually, I enjoyed the engagement with my daughters.

In many instances, memories are much greater than monetary gifts. During their adolescent years, strive to create times and events that are likely to create life long memories.

Make sure you are able to freely express yourself when the family is together. Here's the deal, being goofy before they become teenagers is cool. Once they become teens, being goofy may not be as cool as you think it is. Don't worry; they'll let you know.

During my daughters' elementary school years, I learned about so many things that I obviously missed or they simply were not being taught back in my day. I can remember going to the arts and craft store with my daughters picking out materials to help make dinosaurs, (excuse me, I meant tyrannosaurus and triceratops). I can also remember building an adobe pueblo. Don't feel bad, I didn't know what this was either. This is a model of modern and old communities of Native Americans in the Southwestern Region of the United States. I supported career days. My wife and I were able to take time off to participate in field trips and etc. I even went to my daughters' elementary school to read to their classes. It was important for the teachers and my daughters to see our presence and participation. Moving on to middle (Jr. High) school, and high school, it was important that I supported orchestra events, marching band, or sports events. The big picture is, your presence and support will be embedded in their hearts for the rest of their lives.

In my mind, instilling discipline is a reflection of quality family time. So I'll take this opportunity to talk about teachable moments on discipline. I have heard many elders say, you cannot wait until a child is a teenager to teach them respect, obedience, discipline, responsibility and accountability. The best place to start is when they are young toddlers. This approach may be somewhat old school but I will suggest to you that respect, obedience, discipline, responsibility, and accountability never grows out of style. I have seen modern day parenting where the child actually manipulates and control the parents, intercede into adult conversations, and actually exercise a choice in doing what they want to do. You can no longer discipline children with a belt but a smack on the butt or hand with your hand may sometimes be necessary. If timeouts would have been practiced when I was a child, I probably wouldn't have made it. I would have ran right through that red light. Remember, when you discipline children, do it in love. There are options where a child can learn the easy way or a child can learn the hard way. Sadly, the hard way is represented by probation officers, the Juvenile Justice System, county jails and the prison system. Whatever you fail to teach at home, in all probability, society will take up your slack. Mostly during middle school, I can recall my daughters complaining about how strict we were as parents compared to their friend's parents. Amazingly, as my daughters matured, there was very strong evidence that they had adopted some of the very characteristics that they had previously complained about. They don't like being late for work or school and are usually 15 to 20 minutes early. They can't stand dysfunction and not being organized. They go above and beyond on group projects. They have no problem sitting in front of the class, church, or other. Whatever task they take on (outside of the home), they believe in going above and beyond. For some strange reason, my daughters feel as if they can let off the gas pedal while at home.

Children are very smart. They can do unimaginable things with technology, social media, current trends, their intellect, and etc. There is book smarts and then there is street smarts. There's intelligence and then there's wisdom. There is a void between the two learning mediums; this void is where parents should teach what is commonly called life skills. Life skills are usually associated with managing and living a better quality of life. Life skills help you accomplish your ambitions and live to your fullest potential. Life skills are not taught in high school and they certainly are not taught in college. My father-daughter experiences with identifying life skills that may need developing were only realized after my daughters reached out to me when there was a need or crisis-like situation. As a father, interventions are sometimes needed even when it might initially appear uncomfortable. We must be in tune to what's happening with our daughters beneath their well-camouflaged expressions.

There is no all-inclusive list when considering life skills. A child's needs are based on many factors, factors such as social-economic status, culture, environment, values, morals, and etc. Some of the life skills that may be important include:

- The importance and need for conversation
- How to handle money; personal credit and credit cards; understanding annual percentage rates; loans; savings, budget management
- Dating and romantic relationships
- Car repair and car insurance
- Home ownership and home insurance
- Cooking (can't afford eating out seven days a week for life)
- Health care and health care insurance
- Learning from your mistakes
- Law and order (understanding how your actions can positively or negatively influence law enforcement)
- Retirement planning
- Lease contracts
- Tax laws
- Prioritizing
- Being resourceful

Teaching your daughter the importance of personal decision-making is an essential soft skill. Soft skills are personal attributes that enable someone to interact effectively and harmoniously with other people. How well a child navigates their way through the challenges of life rest largely with how well they are able to make intelligent decisions? One bad decision can have a life-long negative effect on career, happiness, success, health, and relationships. An added element of making bad decisions is the cost, both literally and figuratively that is associated with poor decision-making. What can parents do? First and foremost, parents cannot shield their children from this dilemma. What we can do as parents is to teach our children the importance of making good decisions. You can help your children learn good decision-making by coaching them through decisions.

1. Model good decision-making; good judgement and clear thinking
2. Identify the decision to be made.
3. Seek wise counsel
4. Think of options.
5. Evaluate the options and choose the best one.
6. Put your choice into action and check how it works.

As your children grow older, expand the number of choices you give them. Then, increase the importance of the decisions they can make. With each decision, they should recognize and take responsibility for the consequences of those decisions. Also, retain veto power when needed, but use it judiciously.

Success means different things to different people. We all have hopes and dreams for ourselves, as well as for our children. We want our children to be happy, healthy, secure, and safe. According to scientific study, The Tech Insider, parents of successful children have these things in common, they:

1. Make their children do chores
2. Teach their children social skills
3. Have high expectations
4. Have healthy relationships with each other
5. Have attained higher educational levels

6. Teach their children math early in their childhood or developing stages
7. Develop a healthy relationship with their children
8. Are less stressed
9. Value effort over avoiding failure
10. Have mothers who work
11. Have a higher socioeconomic status
12. Are "authoritative" (power to influence thought, opinion, or behavior) rather than "authoritarian" (relating to favoring blind submission to authority) or "permissive."
13. Teach "perseverance"

While parenting, we are often required to make tough decisions. After disciplining me, I can recall my dear mother telling me, "it was more painful for her than it was for me". At that time, I struggled to understand her pain while I was on the receiving end of the punishment. Once I became a father, I began to fully understand what my mother was saying. Some parenting decisions will be very painful but necessary. Sometimes, it is difficult to be a parent and friend to your child. When faced with this dilemma, being daddy over-ruled everything. I reiterated to my daughters that I was not really interested in becoming their friend until they were completely out of my pockets; meaning, on their own with total financial independence.

Even though my daughters are now young adults, oftentimes we reminisce about family traditions that we've created even though at the time we were just being a loving family to each other. For example, during the Christmas holiday, I like to listen to old school blues and jazz Christmas music. Well, without my urging, they now like to listen to the exact same type of music during the holidays. Needless to say, this warms my heart tremendously.

- Formal education is important; so is social/cultural awareness; i.e. understanding different cultures, places, and things. Expose your daughters to life. Encourage open and honest discussions, no matter how uncomfortable the topics may be. Try to keep your "poker face" on when facing tough and honest Q and A.

- The smallest moments can have the biggest impact on a child's life
- During our daughters' teenage and young adult years, my wife and I encouraged them to have mentors, other than ourselves. Sometimes, having the option to confide in someone else whom you trust is an asset. The mentors they chose were known to us.
- There are times and occasions when you may impact your children without even knowing what you have done until years later.

Community volunteering is an excellent way to help educate your daughter. You can easily find programs that are beneficial and impressionable to young females. There are numerous opportunities to help the elderly, feed the needy at various shelters (particularly during the holiday season), and donating clothes to women and children who reside in shelters. I recall on several occasions which included going to the local convention center to help feed the less fortunate during the holidays. These opportunities were outstanding "teachable moments" and we had fun bonding together while volunteering.

As I talk with other fathers in the barber shop, at church, during work, and in other social settings, the overwhelming question for fathers who are engaged with their children is, did we go too far in giving our children too much? Are we making our children too soft? As a result of giving them so much, are we enabling or inhibiting our children? Honestly, I do not know the answer to these questions. People are different. Every family or situation is different. Perhaps this is one of those parenting decisions where your instincts must guide you. If you ponder the answers to these questions, the one follow up question we must ask ourselves is, are our children ready to confront the world once they leave the friendly confines of our home? In due time, the way our children respond to adversity and their independence will ultimately reveal the answers we are seeking.

It is admirable for a man to take his son fishing, but there is a special place in heaven for the father who takes his daughter shopping.

—John Sinor—

"The difference between school and life? In school, you're taught a lesson and then given a test.

In life, you're given a test that teaches you a lesson."

-Tom Bodett-

Things to Build On:

- In many instances, memories are much greater than monetary gifts.
- I will suggest to you that respect, obedience, discipline, responsibility, and accountability never grows out of style.
- We must be in tune to what's happening with our daughters beneath their well camouflaged expressions.
- Teaching your daughter the importance of personal decision-making is an essential soft skill.
- Some parenting decisions will be very painful but necessary.
- The smallest moments can have the biggest impact on a child's life.
- There are times and occasions when you may impact your children without even knowing what you have done until years later.

Chapter 7 – Education – The Great Equalizer

> *Education is transformational. It changes lives. That is why people work so hard to become educated and why education has always been the key to the American Dream, the force that erases arbitrary divisions of race and class and culture and unlocks every person's God given potential.–*
>
> ***Condoleezza Rice***

Education is key. Education is the cornerstone. The education process starts at home. If you neglect this part of the parenting process, there are potential dire consequences. Refer back to Chapter 4 – Statistics, What Do They Reveal? Why Are They Important? Why Should We Care? Education outside of the home, whether at church or connecting with other social, athletic, or academic clubs, is beneficial to the overall well-being of our children. Elementary, middle school, and high school is where behavioral, social, and academic excellence is formed and re-enforced. Finally, college or an alternative is an absolute must. Please refer to the chart on page 91. Don't expect your child to follow and understand this path to opportunity on their own. Help and guide them to understand the importance of education early in their development. Without education, your child is placed at a distinct disadvantage. Whatever options are pursued, start the process early; your level of intensity early in the process will reduce your level of anxiety in the end.

How does a father approach this awesome task of planning for the college education of his daughters? You plan by way of financial planning, research, collaboration with your wife or daughter's mother, and daughter. Education does not offer any guarantees but it sure does open the door to opportunities. I view college as the foundation for which your life can be built upon.

My wife and I decided against sending our daughters to private schools during their early childhood, primary, and secondary school years. When we purchased our home years ago, the #1 reason for selecting the location was because of the outstanding public school system. At that time, the zoned elementary and high schools were considered "exemplary" schools according to state standards. Where possible, when considering a school choice for your daughter, there is so much criteria to consider. Will the school choice offer enough diversity among the staff and student body? What are the school's results for mandatory testing? How effective is the Parent-Teacher Association? Are parents encouraged to get involved? How prevalent is technology in the school and classroom? Before and after school care options? Campus security? What is the turn-over ratio among teachers? Can you afford to send your child to a private school?

Looking all the way back to when my daughters were in elementary school, whenever there was a parent-student school event or field trip, my wife or I were able to be there to support the school, class, and more importantly, our daughters. We discovered very early that when teachers know that you are engaged in the educational development of your child, somehow, your child is given more attention and greater accountability is expressed from the staff. Each year, in elementary and middle school, usually after parent orientation, I would follow up those visits with the teachers by sending an email, stressing the importance of communication. I would reiterate how important the parent-teacher relationship was to us as parents. My job was to address any concerns involving interactions with authority figures. My daughters' job was to learn. Finally, I would encourage each teacher to contact me immediately if there were any concerns. Whenever it was time for our teacher-parent conferences, I would break down our discussion into four categories:

1. How is my child doing *academically*?
2. How is my child's *behavior*?
3. How is my child doing *socially*?
4. Teacher-student goals

In my mind, if we discussed progress in these four areas, then we pretty much had everything covered. While your child is in a classroom environment, there has to be a learning atmosphere. A child must display respect for authority figures, and they must be able to get along with others.

At the end of each school day, my wife and I would discuss the events of the day with our daughters as we gathered around the dinner table. When asked, how was your day at school, my wife and I would not allow the typical response of "good" without an explanation. We used probing questions to encourage our daughters to give detailed responses. We were seeking genuine answers to our questions. As a parent, you must remain proactive. Generally, children will not inform you of things you need to know until the 11th hour (last minute).

At the end of each school year, beginning in elementary school, each daughter had to give an end of the school year presentation. This presentation involved achievements and accomplishments in the following areas: academics, chores, home disciplinary record, involvement in extracurricular activities, projects, and church involvement. Monetary rewards would be given out or even deducted based on their presentations and their ability to debate or justify their achievements. Basically, my daughters were given the opportunity to acquire spending money for the entire summer. Ironically, of all the things my wife and I did, this was one of the most impactful ideas ever implemented. To this very day, my daughters talk about the positive impact these presentations had on them. I might add, as with most parents, our daughters were also rewarded throughout the school year at the end of each report card period. They received X amount for A's and B's, nothing for C's. During the summer break, my wife established a curriculum involving math, reading and etc. The summer vacation break wasn't just chill time away from learning. Fortunately, for my wife and me, she was the science, technology, engineering, and math (STEM) expert while I was able to offer some level of guidance in English, language, and arts (ELA) department. Ensuring good grades are maintained during primary and secondary schooling, which is a dual responsibility. If tutoring is needed, most schools have before and after school tutoring programs.

As my daughters moved on to high school, we gave them a little more breathing room. The idea here was to help them prepare for their transition from high school to college. Getting up, going to class in college, and studying all boils down to self-discipline. This approach help set the tone for the next level.

Developing the habit of making good grades during these crucial years will go a long way when writing that college acceptance letter. Achieving good grades makes the process so much easier. Bottom line, sending children to college cost money and takes energy and effort. Fortunately for my family, our incomes allowed us to support our daughters' educational dreams. What a blessing for any child to finish their undergraduate degrees with financial help from their parents.

Many institutions of higher learning are now charging $20,000, $30,000, or even $40,000 a year for tuition and fees. This does not include living expenses. According to industry experts, today it is

400% more expensive to go to college in the United States than it was just 30 years ago. The good news is, there are now more scholarship opportunities available than ever before. Securing a scholarship in any form certainly is better than working to pay off a huge student loan. The only warning connected to securing a scholarship is, you've got to do your research. Consider these facts:

- In 2015-16, the average tuition for a state public college costs $9,410. For out of state: $23,893.
- The average tuition for private college in 2015-16: $32,405.
- Over 85% students are receiving some form of financial aid
- In 2014-15, 45% of high school graduates did not file the Free Application for Federal Student Aid
- $122.7 billion worth of scholarships and grants were awarded in 2013-14.
- The average 2016 college student graduated with $37,172 in student loan debt

Resource: "Financial Aid Facts about College in America" by Allison Wignal

As tuition costs climb, saving and planning early for education is one of the most important decisions parents can make. Tax-advantaged 529 savings plans, offered by states, are now one of the most popular options for making sure school expenses will be covered when your child reaches college age.

A 529 plan is a college savings account that's exempt from federal taxes. The plans were introduced in 1996 to help tax payers set aside college expenses for a designated beneficiary.

These plans, named for Section 529 of the federal tax code, often have tax benefits at the state level for in-state residents. This only applies to states that have an income tax. For states who do not offer a 529 Plan, there are alternatives called State College Savings Plan.

Several states have scholarship or grant programs in conjunction with their 529 plans. Each state may offer its own grant and scholarship programs. Some are based on demonstrated financial need, some are based on other types of special characteristics (e.g., grades and/or test scores) and some are focused on particular occupations (e.g., teaching and nursing).

As the leader, fathers should start planning for education early in fatherhood. You may not be able to finance 100% however, you can definitely contribute, even if sacrifices have to be made. One leadership concept I learned during my time in the military was leaders think of others before they think of themselves. I truly believe this is the mindset fathers must have concerning everyone he bears responsibility for.

Please refrain from trying to live or relive your college experience by forcing or attempting to subtly influence your daughter into a college or career choice that she may be opposed to. Educationally, I never pushed my daughters to pursue one particular career over another. I think the key is finding out as soon as possible what it is you are passionate about? What do you enjoy? What are you skilled at doing? What gifts do you possess? What are you talented at doing? What is it that you feel comfortable doing? What is a natural fit for you? Will you be able to support yourself with your career choice? What is the long-term economic forecast for the degree you are pursuing? What is the salary range for your career choice? Is an advanced degree needed? Is a technical school or certification program an option? Which school will prepare you for your desired career? In state/out of state tuition? Can your parents pay for your education? Is a student loan needed? Are scholarships available to help off-set the cost?

Once the choice was made and my daughters were enrolled in college, I couldn't help them with their curriculum issues. Other than finances, the one way I did contribute was through what I call "Dad talks". Periodically my daughters would call or I would call them and we would talk about non-academic related issues. Any problems with your car? How are you getting along with your professors? Did you find a church? Any issues with your dorm room? Are you getting enough rest? Have you found any friends? Don't go someplace and leave an unattended drink. Are you using the "buddy system" when you venture out? Are you focused? As you might imagine, I never had to ask if they needed money; they seized the initiative on that one. Let me emphasize I did not allow my hard earned money for college tuition to be wasted on failing grades.

My daughters decided independently to pursue advanced degrees. During their journey, they have encountered some challenges but life is about overcoming challenges. I am proud of them for not taking the easy path but the path that brings their passion closer to reality. My wife and I have provided moral and financial support up until this point. We hope that if this is something they desire, they will put the final pieces together.

In this chapter, we began with a discussion about education, the great equalizer. I would like to point out that college may not be for everybody and exposure to educational development can be gained through other means besides college. A community college may be the best option. A technical school may fit your daughter's immediate needs. Acquiring a certification may be the best approach to education. Entering some type of armed forces reserves may be the best fit to secure funds for college. Job Corp? Trade school? Even if your daughter foregoes college and decides to enter into the workforce, most jobs have implemented some type of employee continuing education program. A work/school combination may also fit the current situation. There are jobs that will allow you to transition into the workforce without a degree. The point is if your daughter is not considering college as an immediate option, there are other alternatives to achieve a formal education and steady employment.

In summarizing my thoughts, the words below were spoken into my daughters' lives almost nine and five years ago respectively, in their high school yearbooks. After revisiting the yearbook comments, I believe these words are as true today as they were nine and five years ago:

To My Eldest:

Our family, Dad, Mom, and Little Sister are extremely proud of you for achieving the very important milestone of becoming a high school graduate.

As you prepare for the next important milestone (college), we want you to know that you have love and support every step of the way. We want you to enjoy life. We want you to remain focused. We want you to remain disciplined. We want you to follow your dreams as you strive to discover self, achieve success, and pursue happiness.

Life will offer many challenges; your family, the values we attempted to instill, and your faith will always serve as a foundation for every conceivable test life has to offer.

Again, we love you and are very proud of this accomplishment

To My Youngest:

Your family, Dad, Mom, and Big Sister are so very proud of you for achieving the important milestone of high school graduation.
As we reflect on 12 years of elementary, middle school, and high school, we must ask ourselves where the time went. You have set the academic standard for future generations within our family.

Your academic achievements throughout this part of your educational journey have been above and beyond expectations.

It is important for you to remember the value of faith, self-discipline, integrity, character, and remaining humble. Do not forget, you must pass through the clouds before you reach the stars. The two greatest gifts a parent can provide to their child are a solid foundation and wings to fly. It is now time for you to soar.

As you prepare for college and pursue future endeavors, we want you to know that our hearts, thoughts, love, and prayers will always be with you wherever life's journey will take you. Follow your dreams as you strive to discover self, achieve success, and pursue happiness.

"A truly rich man is one whose children run into his arms when his hands are empty."

—Author Unknown—

Things to Build On:

- The education process starts at home.
- Help and guide your daughter to understand the importance of education early in her development.
- Your level of intensity early in the college planning process will reduce your level of anxiety in the end.
- Education does not offer any guarantees but it sure does open the door to opportunities.
- College may not be for everyone, if so, look for viable alternatives
- We discovered very early that when teachers know that you are engaged in the educational development of your child, somehow, your child is given more attention and greater accountability is expressed from the staff.

- As tuition costs increases, saving and planning early for education is one of the most important decisions parents can make.

Unemployment Rate and Earnings by Educational Attainment, 2013

Educational Level	Unemployment Rate (%)	Median Weekly Earning
Doctoral Degree	2.2	1,623
Professional Degree	2.3	1714
Master's Degree	3.4	1329
Bachelor's degree	4.0	1108
Associate's degree	5.4	777
Some college, no degree	7.0	727
High school diploma	7.5	651
Less than a high school diploma	11.0	472
All workers	6.1	827

Note: Data are for persons age 25 and over. Earnings are for full-time wage and salary workers and do not include the self-employed.
Source: U.S. Bureau of Labor Statistics, Current Population Survey

Chapter 8 – Transformation from Young Girls to Young Women; Advice about Boys and Men

> *Men will generally attempt to get away with whatever we are allowed to get away with. If we are held to a standard, we will try our best to meet that standard. We may be more reckless without those standards in place. If a man fails to try to meet certain standards, maybe he's saying you are not worth the effort.*

In the animal kingdom, it is widely known that predators prey on the young, weak, maimed, or the lost (wonderer). As fathers, one of our primary functions is to ensure that our daughters do not fall into any of these vulnerable categories. A greater urgency exist in ensuring our daughters are well prepared if or when we personally know or may have known someone, like (maybe) a former male friend, who was a type of predator by having multiple relational partners back in the day. I am convinced that in the human male species, the hearts of predators can experience change.

I was never in a rush for daddy's little girls to turn into young women. I believe too many parents today want to fast-forward adolescent years, depriving their daughters of the opportunity to truly enjoy and value the childhood experience. A child only has a few years to be a child and has the rest of their lives to enjoy adulthood. Let your daughter enjoy childhood before you rush her into young adulthood.

There were two very distinct events when I knew my daughters and I had crossed that adolescent to young adult threshold. One, I was walking in the mall with my daughters when we were approaching several teenage boys. As they walked past us, I very subtly noticed how they turned to stare or admire my little girls as the three of us were in their personal rear view mirrors. Secondly, one weekend as my wife was preparing to leave for work, she very calmly informed me that one of my daughters has started her menstrual cycle and if something came up, I had to deal with it. Fortunately for me, nothing happened. At that point, I was convinced there was a God.

Communicating. I could have easily talked about communicating in Chapter 5, "The Two Basic Needs – Love and Security"; communication can also be considered a basic need. After giving this a little thought, talking about communicating with your little girl when she's transitioning from pony tails to curvy skinny jeans is crucial. This is also the phase where you are not as important to your daughters as you thought you were. This is the phase where someone who has the exact same thoughts you had when you were a teenager or young adult is jockeying to replace you. If you had difficulty communicating before, you better crack that code now! If you don't, the consequences could be life-changing. To break that barrier, this is the point when real transparency and honesty is to your advantage.

Communication is the lifeline of every father-daughter relationship. A lack of healthy communication creates a distance between parents and children. Effective communication involves not only hearing what others say, but understanding them--and they in return hearing and understanding you. But this is easier said than done. As individuals we each have a unique world view influenced by the way we were raised, our personal experiences, and our environment. Further, we communicate with the benefit of knowing our own motives and intentions, while the recipients of our message don't have that luxury.

Listen first. Communicate in a way that your daughter will understand, you have to dig deep to find out what's on her mind first. That's why listening is so important. Active listening involves asking questions while resisting the urge to judge. When you regularly and skillfully listen to your child, you stay in touch with their reality. Further, you send the message that what's important to them is important to you. Your opinion then carries more weight, because it's based on reality, your child's reality.

Show empathy. When your daughter attempts to tell you her story, try to understand her thought process and see the world from her perspective.

Focus on the positive. Dwelling on the negative in your child is a sure way to breed contempt and close their ears to your own message. Therefore, focus on the positive in your daughter by finding common ground, even if you disagree. Laying this foundation first makes her more willing to hear dissenting or (constructive) critical opinions later.

Be sincere. Be genuine regarding what you appreciate about your daughter. When sharing negative feedback, don't beat around the bush or water it down. Rather, communicate out of a desire to help--and that motive will become obvious. In addition, be willing to sincerely apologize. Apologizing doesn't always mean you're wrong and the other person is right. It just means that you value your relationship more than your ego.

Be specific. Children aren't mind-readers. Therefore, don't just tell them that something bothers you; tell them specifically what needs to change and why. (Of course, if it's negative, communicating with love, tact and grace will make your message easier to accept.

Be respectful. You earn respect when you show it to others first. When speaking, avoid sarcasm and cutting remarks, instead; speak to others the way you want them to speak to you.

Pause when appropriate. Pausing is as simple as taking a moment to stop and think before you speak, especially if you're in a highly emotional state. It may sound simple, but while easy in theory, it's highly difficult to practice consistently.

Be transparent. Transparency doesn't mean sharing everything about yourself to your child all of the time. But it does mean saying what you mean, meaning what you say, and sticking to your values and principles above all else. Know when to yield. Resist the urge to attack every opinion or statement you don't agree with.

Remember, people are emotionally attached to their beliefs. This doesn't mean agreeing with views you're opposed to rather; it's about learning to choose which battles are worth fighting.

Astonishingly, once I accepted the physical changes my daughters were experiencing, communication and engagement actually became fun. Hopefully, my daughters will agree that I was the liberal one. I prided myself in being able to talk to my daughters about any and everything. One of the keys for me was teaching them problem solving and decision-making skills. As we would discuss adult-related issues, I would go out of my way not to tell them how to solve a problem. Ideally, we would discuss the pro and cons of any given situation. I would ask them, based on the pros and cons discussion, if they were led to formulate the best possible decision. As my daughters transitioned from teenagers into young women, I grew to thoroughly enjoy the intellectual conversations with them. Needless to say, the conversations were certainly intriguing. I would submit to you that this is the real test. By that I mean, this is your opportunity to evaluate everything you have been pouring into them from the time they were toddlers in your arms. If you identify any glaring shortcomings, pray you've got time to take corrective measures and hopefully, (at this point), they are even receptive to what you have to say.

I've raised some thoughts about young men and young women with regards to relationships and dating. To capture the true essence of these thoughts, I felt the best way to deliver this smorgasbord of thoughts was in a bullet narrative. So here goes:

- Once they began dating, I often challenged my daughters by asking, how do you know when a young man is interested in a sincere and genuine relationship? I would submit to you that the answer is linked to a person's actions. In other words, when your words are consistently supported by your actions. Say what you mean; mean what you say. If you must constantly ask why someone did not follow through on a commitment or promise. In all likelihood, they are not sincere about the relationship. You might ask, why didn't I mention the heart as another way of recognizing a sincere and genuine relationship?

- Answer – I didn't mention this option because during the formative stages of a sincere and genuine relationship, you may first want to defer to your faith, your dreams, and your understanding of self before you succumb to matters of the heart. A man will only do what you allow him to do! I have often debated this point with members of the opposite sex. Men will always give indicators, the problem lies in young ladies' refusing to acknowledge or accept what the indicators truly reveal. Okay, so he didn't call when he said he would; is this behavior isolated or consistent?

- What are indicators? Indicators are those small things in a relationship that are a tattle tell sign of bigger things to come. As an example, if he never or seldom wants to invite you around his family and friends, that's an indicator. If he doesn't call when he says he will, that's an indicator. If your instincts are constantly troubling you about his actions or a certain behavior, listen to your instincts and your heart.

- Generally, self-confident men are not drawn to women who are overly dependent or needy.

- When dating or if your daughter is looking for "Mr. Right", what makes her think she is ready to become "Miss Right"? So he has to bring certain things to the table, what does she bring? What's on her checklist? Job security? Personality Type? Looks? Education? What are your daughter's long term goals versus his long term goals? Does he have children? Career goals? Does one or the other share too much information about the relationship with their inner circle of friends? Immaturity?

- If the relationship evolves into a seriously dating situation, there is another set of concerns. What is each person smuggling into the relationship? What are the concealed issues? Any history of family violence? Indebtedness? A Lack of money management skills? Different attitude or approach towards sex? Faith preferences? Tithing? Family health issues? Cleanliness? How do you feel about your partner's relationship with friends prior to your relationship? Acceptance & blessings from each other's families? Pets? If shortcomings exist, can you accept them? What about his faith? Ideas on parenting? How to deal with future in-laws?

- I often ask my daughters, what benefits does a male friend have versus a boyfriend?

- When trying to decide if he is the one, your daughter should ask this simple question, if I had a son, would I want my son to emulate this man? In other words, would this man be a positive role model?

- Men chase; women choose

- A daughter's relationship with her father can help to develop the core foundation of how she will interact with boys and ultimately men.

- In considering relationships, your daughter should note how a young man or man interacts with his mother and sisters; in all likelihood, this is a strong indicator of his attitude and treatment of women.

- When dating, does a young man's faith play a prominent role in his life?

- Amazingly, I privately worried more about my daughters as they became adults more than I did when they were adolescents. I am suggesting that the cause of this dilemma was the acknowledgement that my level of protection greatly diminished as they began to make their own decisions.

- I've heard and observed that mothers may be more demanding on daughters while fathers may be more demanding on their sons. As a result, girls may be more drawn to their fathers while sons may be more inclined to be attached to their mothers. Obviously, I am not aware of any hard evidence to support this claim. However, I do personally believe this is applicable to the father-daughter and mother-son relationships. Do opposites really attract?

- As my daughters got older, I tried different approaches to motivate and inspire them. As an example, I often downloaded and sent them what I thought were insightful and inspiring articles via email and text.

- Fathers, when is it time to let go? You will have to rely on the values you have instilled in your daughters.

- A man can respect you and be willing to wait for you if a.) He considers your feelings, and b.) He does not force you into a decision you are opposed to. It's really just that simple.

- Daughters should never ever appear too needy or dependent! Don't give away too much control. There should be a healthy balance between what you give versus what you receive in return and I am not talking about sex! A boyfriend does not have the same rights as a husband.

- If he's indecisive about an important decision, sometimes a little space or a little distance can get his attention or simply reveal something at its core level.

- Why haven't he introduced her to his family?

- Based on their relational agreement, is he reluctant to acknowledge their relationship on social media or with others who are close to him?

- Does his boys know about and respect your daughter?

- Is he concerned about how your daughter feels about things?

- Does he spend money on your daughter while the two of them are out on a date? Does she have to support them?

- This is too basic but let's just throw it out there, does he have a car?

- He may not possess all of the desired attributes at this point in his life but does he have potential? Can she or is she willing to work with what he has?

- Your daughter needs to understand, true love requires maturity. She should be smart about what I'll refer to as the "first love syndrome".

Is your first love a true display of real love or infatuation? If a first love is true, test it for its authenticity. An example of authenticity is can the relationship endure an extended period of separation?

- Planning a life-long relationship with your first love is ideal but be aware, many couples may not end up in a permanent relationship with their first love.

- Remind your daughter that a man should handle her with loving care, just like he would want someone else to treat his sister or another female relative.

I believe that a serious dating commitment is often about timing for men. Let me explain. During the course of dating, it is not uncommon for men to meet quality, marriage conscious, or virtuous young ladies. There's nothing wrong with these women during these dating escapades; the issue is the immaturity of the male as he is going through his experimentation phase. As a quality marriage conscious young lady, you've got to be aware of what is happening. It's not you! Once a woman recognizes this for what it is, she has to take the necessary steps to protect herself. If he comes to his senses and realizes your value early on, he will not allow you to escape. If he has a problem with seriously dating, again, recognize the situation for what it is. I would argue that most young ladies enter into relationships with the mindset of, I can handle any relationship. Just remember, emotionally, you were created different.

When I would conjure up conversations with my daughters about boyfriends and dating, I would initially challenge them with a question. The question is, what is the difference between boyfriends versus a male friends? My thinking was if you can master or articulate the answer to this question, then you were probably mature enough to handle a relationship with someone of the opposite sex. If you could not properly articulate a response to this question, it at least provoked a thought and a message was sent to ponder the implications of the question. A little subtle parental pressure never hurt.

While discussing relationships with my daughters, I would ask, how do you know if a young man is serious about you? A mature woman might reasonably answer this easy question. However, a young impressionable young lady may struggle with an answer. I would submit to you that the best possible answer is when his words are supported by his actions. If he says he's going to call, he calls as promised. If he says he cares for you, how is that care expressed? If you are ever placed in a compromising situation, is your decision respected? If he often struggles with backing up his words with actions, this strongly indicates that he does not take you seriously. You are probably being played. Both parties in the relationship must be held accountable.

When dating, there will be "seasons of aloneness". How will your daughter handle this situation? A seasons of aloneness is described as a time when finding a suitable companion is taking too long or when she is in between an ex-boyfriend and a potential boyfriend. This situation can be disastrous if it is mishandled. First and foremost, the two worst reactions to this situation are to rush into another relationship with someone else too soon or to lower your standards without realizing that desperation has set in. Should your daughter encounter this situation and hopefully she confides in you, my advice is to tell her to connect with family and sincere friends, those who love her and will be honest with her. Also, she should learn to love; reassuring where she stands with her faith, exercise, attend outings with friends, reading, meditating, or finding a new hobby. Before she should consider getting back into the dating game again, she needs to make sure she is past that vulnerable stage. Remember, predators know when you are wounded.

Every family that has daughters, nieces, and female cousins need a gentle enforcer. For clarity, a gentle enforcer is someone who expresses concerns, love, and has the best interest of female family members in mind. Before anyone misinterprets what I am saying, I am not referring to someone who is capable of dishing out verbal or physical threats. I am suggesting that on the subject of dating and male relationships, a gentle enforcer is a male family member who is trusted, respected, and is a mentor and role model. I welcomed this role on behalf of the female relatives. Whenever my nieces and daughters thought they were ready to seriously date someone, I was the trusted family member to give them "the down low" or the thumbs up on what I thought about this particular person. This was usually done after discussions with my nieces. Sometimes, their male friends would be forewarned (by them) prior to a family event and sometimes they were subtly interrogated, without the young man's knowledge or consent. It's important for young men to know they are accountable.

It's important for young men to know there are family members who care about the well-being of female family members. It's important for young men to know that there are standards and expectations. It's important that these type of interactions occur face to face. It was interesting. To this very day, I accept this assignment with great pride.

"The reason why daughters love their Dad the most is…that there is at least one man in the world who will never hurt her".

—Anonymous—

"If you are a marriage conscious young lady, you should not invest more than two years into a relationship. If he cannot decide if you are the one within that time frame, then it may be time for you to move on. You've got to re-invest or start the process all over again".

—Fanetta Dickens—

Things to Build On:

- A child only has a few years to be a child and has the rest of their lives to enjoy adulthood.
- Communication is the lifeline of every father-daughter relationship.
- One of the keys for me was teaching them problem solving and decision-making skills.
- It's important for young men to know there are family members who care about the well-being of female family members.
- A daughter's relationship with her father can help to develop the core foundation of how she will interact with boys and ultimately men
- Remind your daughter that a man should handle her with loving care, just like he would want someone else to treat his sister or another female relative.

Chapter 9 – Building a Legacy

> *Be careful; as a father, you can establish the wrong type of legacy.*

After following my instincts to add this chapter, those same instincts led me to drill down further to ask a question. Why is it so rare for men to discuss, understand, and take the necessary steps toward leaving a legacy? As I reflect on my conversations with other fathers and men in general, leaving a legacy is a topic that is seldom discussed. I believe thoughts and conversations about your legacy are generated from someplace much deeper within us. Contemplating your legacy does not occur without serious thought, conversation, and reflection. The foundation and the desire to leave a legacy for those you love and care for is formed as a result of numerous factors. What impact does your values, morals, and beliefs have on developing your views towards leaving a legacy? Did you have a loving relationship with your grandparents, other elders in the family, and friends? Do you value family? Did you have an appreciation for others who paved the way for your success? Have you contemplated your purpose for being here? Were you taught to celebrate, honor, and appreciate causes in your life that may be larger than you? Have you given any consideration to how you want to be remembered? The road to building a legacy begins early in life and starts with the way you treat those with whom you come in contact with along the way. I would share with you that thoughts of leaving a legacy are deep-rooted in your sense of fatherhood, purpose, maturity, wise decision-making, and the ability to establish vision in your life. When you focus on the seriousness of fatherhood and life, you are more inclined to place emphasis on the more meaningful aspects of life and living. The life and spirit of the holistic man does not end when he departs this earth. The holistic man impacts the life of others long after his natural life has ended.

Legacy is about life and living. It's about learning from the past, living in the present, and building for the future. I believe that each generation should have a better opportunity than their parent's generation. Hypothetically, if I had an annual income of $100,000, I want my daughters to make $150,000. If I couldn't afford or have the opportunity to pursue my true passion, I want them to have the opportunity to do so. If I received a good education, I want my daughters to receive a great education. If I was able to send my daughters to an in state public or private institution of higher learning, I want them to be able to send their children to a college of choice anywhere in the nation. If I was able to have a six-month salary cushion in the bank, I want them to have a one – year salary cushion in the bank for themselves and/or their families. You get the picture.

The Temptations said, "Papa was a rolling stone, wherever he laid his hat was his home! And when he died, all he left us was alone!" A family on this side of town & another family on the other side of town; children that are known to others only when it is revealed at your memorial service; multiple children by multiple mothers; dishing out physical and mental abuse; avoiding parental and financial responsibilities! A large number of households were without a male role model; the female head of household had to be mother and father! This is how some fathers of the Silent Generation rolled (my father's generation) during the 50s and 60s. As a result of the non-ideal legacy that had been handed down to me, I made a vow. My vow was to break the chain. Whatever fatherly contributions were absent in my life, I was determined to be there for my children. In fact, I confided in my wife and shared with her that as long as God allowed me to live, my daughters would never call another man daddy. I was determined to be the only daddy they would ever know. Be careful. As a father, you can create the wrong type of legacy.

Unfortunately, many of us are so busy struggling to survive day to day or month to month, we don't have very much room to squeeze in concerns about our legacy. Your legacy through your children is not just limited to financial well-being or material things. Your legacy involves helping others, imparting wisdom, protecting and respecting the family name, ancestral story-telling, how others will remember you, and your contribution to society and others.

Confirmation about what you will pass along to your daughters starts much earlier than you may think. Eventually your daughter's actions will reveal so much about what they have retained, particularly about whether or not they have demonstrated some of the values you have attempted to instill in them. For example, at an early age, as early as elementary school, I witnessed my eldest daughter befriend a special needs child during a field trip. To this day, my eldest daughter has developed a passion for social consciousness and how misfortunes impact the lives of the less fortunate. Also, as she matured, I grew proud of the way she persevered during some graduate school challenges. I also witnessed my youngest take on a mentoring and tutoring role for younger nieces and cousins. Also, when we decided it was okay for her to pursue part-time employment while in high school, my youngest took the initiative and found several jobs without help from her parents. During these moments, I begin to realize that "yes", they were getting it. You may think they are not watching and listening, but I assure you, they are.

Another way of considering the importance of a legacy is by remembering how all of us have benefitted from the commitments and sacrifices of others before us. We achieved what we have because the way was paved for us by great grandparents, grandparents, parents, aunts, uncles, or friends. One of the best ways to honor those who have contributed towards our success is to honor them through the way we live our lives. Whatever parents, relatives, and mentors have taught you, represent them well.

Another way of viewing this is, whatever your life style choices are, would the people who had faith in you be pleased with who you have become and what you represent? As quoted by my late mother, Ora M. Peterson, "A good name is hard to find." Protecting and honoring the family name is a form of continuing your family's legacy.

Before we (fathers) can begin to build a legacy for our children, are we really in tune with who our children really are? When others speak of millennials and Generation Z/Boomlets, do we really know and understand where they are coming from? Aside from parenting, each generation has been impacted by the world, events, social dynamics, technology, politics, societal attitudes, religion, and etc.; in ways that are beyond the reach of family influence. Most parents today are Baby Boomers, Generation X'ers, and some early Millennials. Our children are known to be (late) Millennials and Generation Z/Boomlets. If truth be told, sometimes parents struggle with trying to connect with their children because their thinking, behavior, and attitudes are vastly different from that of their parents. In an attempt to offer some insight, the chart on page 112 was created by Dr. Jill Novak from The *Six Living Generations in America*.

It is difficult to begin building a legacy if there is a lack of understanding of who you are building it for. Consider the core issues regarding the recipients of your legacy. What motivates them? Where do their interest lay? How do they see themselves? What do they value? What areas of life do they respond to responsibly versus areas they respond to irresponsibly? Consider what can and cannot be entrusted. Going forward, how do you want to motivate and encourage your children? Knowing the answers to these or similar questions should impact the type of legacy you are considering leaving for your children.

You brought nothing into this world and I assure you will take nothing with you when you die. So when you die, what will you leave behind? Something memorable? Something impactful? Debt? Will your death create confusion? After a period of mourning, will your death create warm and happy heart-felt memories and security for your love ones? Will your children want to pass on whatever you instilled in them? How many lives did you positively or negatively impact? How many people did you hurt? Have you scarred someone for life? Will others be able to say you made a positive difference in their lives? Surely, we all have made mistakes; once recognized, do all that is within your power to make it right.

Your daughter will most likely become a wife and mother; what will she carry over in the next phase of her life that she received from you? As a father, I want to challenge you today that if you have not thought about what legacy you will leave behind, today is a good day to change all of that.

As an extension of the legacy discussion, are your personal and legal affairs in order? God forbid, if something were to happen to you, would your child, wife, or the mother of your child have to endure an unnecessary legal challenge because you neglected your responsibilities in this area? Do you have a will? Do you have life insurance? Does your family know where to find critical documents if there was a need? Is there a living trust? Have you identified a legal guardian? Have you sat down and had a discussion with anyone in the event of your death? When we are young, we assume that we will live forever. However, we simply do not know when our time on earth will end. Many of us may be uncomfortable with this type of planning and discussion but nonetheless, it would be in our best interest to get our affairs in order.

For varying reasons, many of us simply do not see the value of leaving a legacy. The reasons may vary; lack of vision, limited resources, or lack of education and understanding on this matter.

Apathy? Maybe, no one ever talked to us about the importance of leaving a legacy. My wife and I have decided to invest in the education of our two children and our yet to be born grandchildren. Educationally, we want our daughters to have a better opportunity at life than we did. We believe that education is the absolute key to opportunities for success in the future. Armed with their education and upbringing, we hope and pray that future generations will become trailblazers for making the world and the lives of others better. I am constantly reminded by my wife that as we transition further into our golden years and develop the need to be looked after; girls will always be there for you.

Establishing a foundation for creating a legacy involves having critical conversation with your child(ren). Critical conversation involves challenging them to be thoughtful, reflective, considerate, and conscience of themselves, their surroundings, and the world we live in. If you were to ask your children the following questions, how would they respond?

- Who am I?
- Where am I from?
- Why am I here?
- What can I do?
- Where am I going?

What is the end gain of leaving a legacy for your children? It's really not about remembering who we were as parents; it's about making the world we live in a much better place through our children, more so than it was when we inherited our rightful places from our parents and forefathers.

"Children's children are a crown to the aged, and parents are the pride of their children".

Proverbs 17:6 (NIV)

"The meaning of life is to find your gift. The purpose of life is to give it away".

Pablo Picasso

"Sometimes the poorest man leaves his children the richest inheritance."

—Ruth E. Renkel—

Things to Build On:

- The holistic man impacts the life of others long after his natural life has ended.
- I believe that each generation should have a better opportunity to achieve success in life more than their parent's generation.
- Your daughter will most likely become a wife and mother. What will she carry over in the next phase of her life that she received from you?
- Many of us may be uncomfortable with this type of planning and discussion. Nonetheless, it would be in our best interest to get our affairs in order.

Generation Y/Millennials	Generation Z/Boomlets
• Born between 1981* and 2000*. • Aka "The 9/11 Generation" "Echo Boomers" • They are nurtured by omnipresent parents, optimistic, and focused. • Respect authority • Falling crime rates. Falling teen pregnancy rates. But with school safety problems; they have to live with the thought that they could be shot at school, they learned early that the world is not a safe place. They schedule everything. • They feel enormous academic pressure. • They have great expectations for themselves. • Prefer digital literacy as they grew up in a digital environment. Have never known a world without computers! They get all their information and most of their socializing from the Internet. Prefer to work in teams. • Envision the world as a 24/7 place; want fast and immediate processing. • They have been told over and over again that they are special, and they expect the world to treat them that way. • They do not live to work, they prefer a more relaxed work environment with a lot of hand holding and accolades.	• Born after 2001* • In 2006 there were a record number of births in the US and 49% of those born were Hispanic; this will change the American melting pot in terms of behavior and culture. • There are two age groups right now: • **(a)** Tweens-Age 8-12 years old. • There will be an estimated 29 million tweens by 2009. • $51 billion is spent by tweens every year with an additional $170 billion spent by their parents and family members directly for them. • **(b)** Toddler/Elementary school age. • 61% of children 8-17 have televisions in their rooms. • 35 % have video games. • 14 % have a DVD player. • 4 million will have their own cell phones. They have never known a world without computers and cell phones. • With the advent of computers and web based learning, children leave behind toys at younger and younger ages. As children reach the age of four and five, old enough to play on the computer, they become less interested in toys and begin to desire electronics such as cell phones and video games.

	They are savvy consumers and they know what they want and how to get it and they are over-saturated with brands.

Www.marketingteacher.com/the-six-living-generations-in-America/Dr. Jill Novak, University Phoenix, Texas A&M University.

Chapter 10 – The Importance of Faith and Biblical Principles

Without a doubt, I was the beneficiary of my mother's prayers and the faith-based values she had instilled in me; consequently I wanted my daughters to have the same foundation I had.

Let me begin this chapter by saying, I am respectful of all faiths. It is not my position to be critical of anyone's faith, belief or non-belief. Having read the previous nine chapters, perhaps it is easy to recognize where I stand on this issue. Throughout the previous chapters, I have periodically quoted scripture from the Bible. I did so to help illustrate various points. The intended purpose of this chapter is not to try to convince you to abandon your belief or to convert your belief into mine. The purpose is to simply share with each reader how my faith has positively impacted my ability to raise my children.

When I was growing up in my mother's house, going to church was simply not an option. Sunday School, singing in the Youth Choir, Vacation Bible School, and Youth Church (back then we called it Baptist Training Union) was a way of life. Once I left my mother's house, I rarely went to church for a number of years. My attitude about church changed when I became a father. Thankfully, I was wise enough to know and understand how vital it was for me to recommit myself to my faith once I became a father. While I was living the life of a modern day Prodigal Son, I never forgot about my upbringing and how fervently my mother had prayed for me. Without a doubt, I was the beneficiary of my mother's prayers and the faith-based values she had instilled in me. Consequently, I wanted my children to have the same foundation I had.

What influence did the church have on me as a child? For starters, a solid foundation for life was established as a result of attending church. I learned to have reverence for God. I learned to be respectful towards others. More importantly, church is where I first felt the pressure of not wanting to disappoint any of the elders whom had taken the time to take on an interest in me. Church is where the foundation of discipline was re-enforced. Church is where I first experienced love outside of my immediate family. Church is where, to this day, lifelong friendships and relationships were nurtured.

At my church today, one of our core values is "The Next Generation - The Future Is Now". Eagles are men and women who are 50+ in age. One of the "implied" roles for men who are "Eagles" is to connect with and help develop young men. This is particularly important because my Pastor cannot personally and regularly impart into the lives of each and every man. To help with the Connect Process, Eagles are to reinforce, one man at a time, what is being taught from the pulpit.

In discussing and writing about *Raising Cougars and Bears (Parenting Daughters - A Father's Perspective)*, I am striving to fulfill my part in this endeavor. I think it is essential that men help pour into the lives of men. Iron does sharpen iron. And, as my Pastor reminds us, "Men go first".

God holds parents responsible for the upbringing of children; not grandparents, not schools, not the state, not youth groups, not peers and friends. Although each of these groups may influence children, the final duty rest with the parents, and particularly with the father, whom God has appointed to lead and serve the family. Two things are necessary for the proper teaching of children: a right attitude and foundation. An atmosphere reeking with destructive criticism, condemnation, unrealistic expectations, sarcasm, intimidation, and fear will provoke a child to anger. In such an atmosphere, no sound teaching can take place.

The positive alternative would be an atmosphere rich in encouragement, tenderness, patience, listening, affection, and love. In such an atmosphere, parents can build into the lives of their children.

I'm sure many of us have different and wide-ranging views with respect to how faith plays into the life of our children. As a youngster, growing up in a rural part of the Deep South, I was a definite challenge to my mother to remain on the straight and narrow. Oftentimes, I would engage in adolescent activity that would certainly test the rule of law but for some reason, I never crossed the line she had established. Okay, maybe once or twice! To this day, I am convinced that my mother's prayers and her hands on approach to single-parenting was key to keeping me out of trouble. As previously mentioned, and even though I strayed from church for a number of years, the image I had of her faith, sacrifice, commitment, and dedication never left me. When I became a father for the first time at the age of 33, I immediately knew that I needed to mimic what I had witnessed my Mother doing for me. Even though at the time, I was still experiencing growth with my spiritual development and maturity, the faith-based foundation and seed had been planted by my mother. But not only had the seed and foundation been planted in me, I can attest to the fact that faith and prayer worked for me and on me.

Once you make the decision to involve your child in church, allow them the opportunity to participate in a ministry or other faith-based activities. Children who engage in ministry form likeminded relationships, develop a spiritual education, and are safe and protected while participating. One word of caution: as a parent, make sure you also participate periodically. Talk to the leaders, volunteer, and serve so that you will know first-hand what is going on. If you identify a problem, also be prepared to offer a solution. This would be a win-win-win situation for all involved parties, meaning you, your child, and the church. The children would benefit immensely from seeing a father engaged in the well-being of the entire group.

Simply put, my wife and I intentionally placed our daughters in a faith based environment because we wanted them to know, understand, and value the significance of faith in their lives.

In fact, when deciding on a place to worship, our first choice had more to do with our daughters than us. We wanted to ensure our children had an opportunity to grow spiritually at a church where the teachings were real and relevant to everyday life. We felt this was the right approach for our children to help overcome the struggles of modern-day society. Once they became young adults and moved away, either temporarily or semi-permanently, we had no control of their actions in this regard. We did have the comfort and peace of mind that the foundation had been set. When they left for college, we were rewarded with an affirmation that they had decided to seek out a local church in their college towns.

Pray for your Children

Parents should pray for their children's spiritual as well as physical health and well-being. Parents should ask God to help guide their children in all that they say and do. Parental prayer should be a daily reminder to parents that God has entrusted them with the rearing and training of their children. Parental prayer is an integral part of the loving relationship parents have for their children.

Praying for your children is not a privilege that we have as parents, it is a necessity. Our children live in a tough world. Each day our children are subjected to literally thousands of offensive images and words. Our children also face an enormous amount of peer pressure to become part of what is considered normal by the world's standards. Without prayer, our children will not be able to stand against the insurmountable odds that they will face from childhood until they leave this world.

As a father, pray for your children. Pray over them, pray with them, and be thankful for them. Don't wait until a crisis arises before you feel compelled to pray; pray in season and pray out of season. Pray consistently and constantly. Let your children know that you pray for them daily. Just as you have been appointed an earthly father, take comfort in knowing that we all have a Heavenly Father who sent his son Jesus Christ, our Lord and Savior, to show us the way.

"The righteous lead blameless lives; blessed are their children after them"
—Proverbs 20:7 (NIV) —

The Law of Divine Reciprocity - A Guiding Principle

I want to talk about a topic that you may or may not be familiar with and how it can influence your child's view of life and the ability to interact with people. The topic is what is recognized as "the Law of Divine Reciprocity".

The Law of Reciprocity is a component of what is commonly called Universal Laws. Also referred to as Spiritual Laws or Laws of Nature, some believe they are the unwavering and unchanging principles that govern every aspect of the universe and are the means by which our world and the entire cosmos continues to exist, thrive and expand.

If you were to further study each of the Universal Laws, you could surmise that each is interconnected to a perfectly constructed group of unwavering and enduring "Laws", each working in "perfect harmony" 100% of the time, serving to provide a specific outcome.

You reap what you sow. Do unto others as you would have them to do unto you. Treat others the way you want to be treated. To get respect, you must give respect. It is better to give than to receive. While considered time-honored cliques, these statements provide insight and are commonly connected to the Law of Divine Reciprocity. I would suggest to you that our forefathers were spiritually connected to the importance of this belief. I believe that going forward, it is just as crucial today as it was in the past for our children to understand how the Law of Divine Reciprocity is vital to our faith, values, beliefs, relationships, and how we respond to the challenges life has to offer.

There is a Law of Divine Reciprocity. You give; God gives in return. When you plant a seed, the ground yields a harvest. That is a reciprocal relationship. The ground can only give as you give to the ground. You put money in the bank and the bank returns interest. This is reciprocity.

But many of us want something for nothing when it comes to the things of God. We know it does not work that way in the world's system. Yet we always expect God to send us blessings when we have not invested in the kingdom of God. If we are not investing our time, talent, commitment, and our money, why do we expect blessings? How can we expect God to honor our desires when we have not honored his command to give? Prosperity begins with investment.

In relationships, reciprocity is the basis of trust and legitimate power. The principle is that others will reciprocate kindly based upon the way you treat them. The world gives you what you give to the world. Relationships essentially work in the same manner.

The Bible reminds us that; "Whoever sows sparingly will also reap sparingly, and whoever sows generously will also reap generously.... And God is able to make all grace abound to you, so that in all things at all times, having all that you need, you will abound in every good work." [Bible citation]

Reciprocity isn't always instantaneous, therefore persistence is vital. Even if you've found yourself saying "I've tried that and it doesn't work", don't give up! At the proper time you will reap a harvest. By understanding and using the power of reciprocity, you can improve your relationships and avoid mistakes that can permanently damage your relationships. In life and work, you get what you give.

When establishing a teachable foundation for your children, understanding and applying the Law of Divine Reciprocity is a good foundation. I am not advocating this as an absolute method of teaching. However, the Law of Divine Reciprocity can be used as a platform to promote giving, good behavior, respect, tolerance, responsibility, self-control, honesty, integrity, perseverance, gratitude, and role modeling.

Just to highlight a few teachable lessons, the bible re-enforces:

- *"Listen, my sons, to a father's instruction; pay attention and gain understanding"*. **Proverbs 4:1 (NIV)**

- *"Train up a child in the way he would go, And when he is old he will not depart from it"*. **Proverbs 22:6 (NKJV)**

- *"Children obey your parents in the Lord, for this is right"*. **Ephesians 6:1 (NKJV)**

- *"As a father shows compassion or his children, so the Lord shows compassion to those who fear him"*. **Psalms 103:13 (NKJV)**

Finally, as I reflect on the journey and where it all began, in the deep, rural south, in an impoverished neighborhood called River Bottom, I am amazed at what God can do. It started with a dream, with a vision. It is possible to take what is perceived as the worst of beginnings and circumstances and turn that situation into a process that benefits, and encourages others. Your circumstances, wherever you begin your journey will not hinder you from dreaming. You can connect with the very thing you have been dreaming about. As a man, as a parent, if you have been dreaming about a better life for you and your children, your dreams are within reach. If you have been struggling to rise above a challenging situation, you can achieve that. Never, ever give up on your dreams. Others are waiting to be blessed by you.

On Sunday, December 31, 2017, the last Sunday of Calendar Year 2017, I was listening to a sermon by my Pastor, Pastor Terrence H. Johnson entitled "I Dare You to Dream Again". As I listened, I reflected on how your dreams, vision, and ideas can impact your development as a father. The following key points encouraged me:

- God's blueprint for our lives start with dreams, imagination; an idea
- Imagine yourself doing (_____); Dream about it.
- Critics and circumstances will be encountered with your dreams
- Don't let the opinions of others shape your life
- Expectations are based on your view
- When you change your view, you are able to see what you can accomplish
- Sometimes the process may not feel good
- Learn to value and recognize the process
- People will be blessed through you via your dreams
- Your dreams will help someone to be set free
- Hope and encouragement results from your dreams
- You are not alone; God is always with you

I wanted to spend my final thoughts talking about brokenness; brokenness as it relates to relationships, rejection, and betrayal. It occurred to me that many of us may have endured pain and suffering as a result of our relationship or lack of a relationship with our biological fathers. It also occurred to me that old wounds could potentially be opened or reopened as a result of this book.

Oftentimes, in father-daughter or parent-child relationships, hurt, pain, rejection, and disappointment can impact a person's life for a lifetime.

One thing I do know, you cannot hold on to these feelings of disappointment forever. At some point you must make a decision to move forward with your life. I am not a counselor but I would suggest that overcoming relational disappointments is akin to overcoming the death of a love one. No one can tell you how to grieve. No one can tell you how long to grieve. The one thing we should be able to agree on is that you cannot grieve the loss of a loved one forever. Overcoming relational pain with a parent can be viewed in this light. Talking about your pain and disappointment is fine. Reflecting on it at times is fine. Using your pain and disappointment as a testimony to help others is fine. Talking, reflecting, and using your situation as a testimony is helpful and therapeutic. At some point in the process, you must live your life to the fullest. You need to continue to move forward.

The solution can never come from our own efforts or will, but comes only from our faith in God. Only when we recognize our need for God are we able to take our eyes off ourselves and focus them on God and Jesus Christ. Only when we stop thinking about ourselves and start thinking about the sacrifices that were made for us individually can we begin to heal. Only when we admit our needs and invite God to enter our life is when he will make us whole. Only when we confess that we are broken can God make us into what He wants us to be. Once we let go of ourselves and place God at the center of our lives, then everything else falls into place.

I have grown to understand that the forgiveness of others is important to the healing process. However, forgiveness does not substitute a relationship. Holding on to bitterness or nursing a grudge only poisons our own spirit. Yes, we may have been truly wronged, and the pain is real, but there is freedom in forgiveness.

Forgiveness is a gift we can give because it was given to us by the Lord Jesus Christ.

"The Lord is close to the broken-hearted and saves those who are crushed in spirit" **Psalm 34:18 (NKJV)**

Parenting is intentional. Parenting is assuming responsibility. Parenting is submitting to a cause and a purpose that is larger than you.

Things to Build On:

- Without a doubt, I was the beneficiary of my mother's prayers and the faith-based values she had instilled in me. Consequently, I wanted my children to have the same foundation I had.
- Oftentimes, in father-daughter or parent-child relationships, hurt, pain, rejection, and disappointment can impact a person's life for a lifetime.
- God holds parents responsible for the upbringing of children; not grandparents, schools, the state, youth groups, nor peers and friends.
- Praying for your children is not a privilege that we have as parents; it is a necessity.

A Father's Love

A father is respected because He
gives his children leadership…
Appreciated because
He gives his children care…
Valued because
He gives his children time…
Loved because
he gives his children the one thing
they treasure most – himself.

Unknown

That's A Wrap

As I was writing this book, I tried to make a concerted effort to be as forthright as possible and, more importantly, minimize inconsequential conversation. Inconsequential conversation is what I describe as inserting unnecessary verbiage (content fillers) into the book's content. This is why each chapter is somewhat brief, direct, and to the point. I made this concerted effort because I wanted to seriously make the attempt to connect with men. Connecting with men include understanding the idea that we may not feel as if we have a lot of time to read. This may be particularly true when our reading choices are not work-related. As a result, when we do engage in reading, the goal is to produce quality and engaging reading material. Hopefully, my efforts to avoid inconsequential conversation will result in encouraging men to take the plunge and start reading about this topic. I am also optimistic that the ladies will understand and appreciate my efforts. Then again, my attempt at being direct could very easily be viewed as a preference for the ladies as well.

After my first book release, *Aspiring Professionals How to Enhance Your Professional Performance and Productivity*, I am proud to release my second publication, *Raising Cougars and Bears (Parenting Daughters – A Father's Perspective)*.

I am truly excited about the opportunity to pursue my second publication. Why did I choose to write about *Raising Cougars and Bears (Parenting Daughters – A Father's Perspective)*? For starters, I wanted to write about something in which I had in-depth knowledge. Secondly, even though this idea had been rolling around in my head and deep within my spirit for quite some time, I had to wait on the principle characters (my daughters) to see what twists and turns they would take towards their advanced degrees. Supporting and encouraging my daughters as they worked towards completing their advanced degrees and starting their careers was extremely important to me. Finally, I have decided to write about issues that hopefully and prayerfully have a positive and motivating impact on the lives of others. Inspiring and motivating others is my goal. As an author, my ultimate goal is for each reader to:

- Be encouraged and inspired
- Learn something they did not previously know
- Re-enforce something they already knew
- Reflect on what was revealed in the book; expressing a satisfactory nod of approval
- Express a desire to share this reading experience with others

Ultimately, I am driven by the need to exercise my love for writing and my desire to help others through the prism of my various experiences. My perspective of this subject matter is based on three principles: a biblical foundation; the guiding values, principles, and morals that were instilled in me and my application of the realities and challenges of fatherhood.

Finally, no matter who you are, the reality is as fathers, we want and desire the same things for the children we love. Those same things include happiness, success, security, safety, good health, and opportunity.

Appendix 1
Bilateral Contractual Agreement Between Dad and Mom (Party #1) and Eldest and Youngest Daughter (Party #2)

1) Purpose:
   A. What is the purpose of this bilateral contractual agreement between _____(father),_____(mother), _____ (eldest daughter),_____ and _____(youngest daughter)? The purpose of this bilateral contractual agreement is to 1.) Reestablish expectations and clarity for all family members who will reside in Dad's and Mom's household effective May 2016. This is particularly important because of the amount of time that has elapsed since all four (4) family members resided in the same household, 2.) Acknowledge that since the departures & temporary relocation of _____ in 2011 and _____ in 2012, the two of you have become adults. This bilateral contractual agreement is your parent's way of acknowledging and encouraging your transition into full and independent adulthood, and 3.) Your parent's newly-attained retirement status reinforces how important it is for the both of you to gain 100% independence while also reiterating the need for all decisions to be fugal, thoughtful, purposeful, efficient, and wise. During the length of this bilateral contractual agreement, you will be permitted to reside at _____ if you continue to abide by this agreement. 3% of your full-time or part-time salary will be designated for contribution towards living expenses i.e. rent, utilities, food, medical insurance, and dental insurance. Your parents ultimate goal is for the both of you to be loved, happy, healthy (spiritually and physically), independent, and prosperous (financially and relationally).

2) In this space, please state your immediate goal(s) & your timeline for attaining that goal?

    A. _____

    B. _____

3) In this space, please list some milestones or bench-markers or indicators that will reflect that you are on track to achieving your ultimate goal(s) (see examples in paragraph below).

    A. _____

    B. _____

    C. Example
- a) Prepare & pass the State's Teacher's Certification
- b) Prepare & pass the Medical College Admission Test (MCAT)
- c) Gain acceptance to medical school. Prayerfully, target an in- state school to take advantage of the Hazelwood Act and scholarship
- d) Save $__ within 18 months
- e) Research & secure student loans for Med School
- f) Apply & secure suitable teaching employment by September
- g) 2018
- h) During employment, continue to work towards earning an EdD
- i) Find a suitable balance between family, studying, & friends
- j) Remain employed while pursuing an advanced degrees
- k) Establish a budget to alleviate living financially from day to day or week to week

4) In the space below, identify, if any, what additional resources that are *thought* to be needed from Mom & Dad?

   A. A new, 100% financed _____ automobile _____
   B. A 75% - 100% debt-free undergrad degree from the universities of your choice
   C. _____
   D. _____

5) Attitude

   A. Philippians 2:14-15 - Do all things without grumbling or questioning, that you may be blameless and innocent, children of God without blemish in the midst of a crooked and twisted generation, among whom you shine as lights in the world.
   B. Ephesians 6:1-3 - Children, obey your parents in the Lord, for this is right. "Honor your father and mother" (this is the first commandment with a promise), "that it may go well with you and that you may live long in the land."
   C. We respect the fact that you are adults however, Mom & Dad will always remain "authority" figures. With regard to becoming an adult, total financial independence does foster friendship rather than parent-ship.
   D. Communicating has priority over attitude
   E. In "plain text", when your parents identify something that should be done, do it without attitude.

6) Home Management

   A. We take pride in owning our home, this is a noteworthy accomplishment & investment. We think our home is lovely & is a reflection of who we are. Another way of looking at our home is eventually it is a $ ____ (+) asset for the both of you.

B. Your bedrooms must remain presentable while doors are open. Clutter & uncleanliness are not acceptable with regard to the upkeep of your bedrooms. Note: The purpose of this stipulation is to emphasize the fact that the two of you are now adults. Adults demonstrate responsibility in owning, maintaining, & caring for whatever it is you work to acquire.
C. Respect all bedrooms before entering by "knocking first"
D. Your bathroom must be cleaned at least every other day. We should not have to scramble to clean anything whenever guests may unexpectedly stop by.
  (1) Define clean:
    (2) Toilet cleaned w/brush & pine sol
    (3) Sink cleaned
    (4) Floor swept & mopped
    (5) Trash emptied daily
    (6) Shower cleaned each Friday
    (7) Place used towels in laundry area (not kept in individual rooms).

7) Kitchen

  A. Whoever cooks is automatically relieved from washing dishes.
  B. Dishwashing responsibilities will be rotated weekly between ____ & ____.
  C. Mom & Dad will not wash dishes except when they simply want to or dishwashing is negotiated
  D. No (zero) dirty dishes overnight.
  E. When dishes are washed, the floor will be swept & all counter tops will be wiped cleaned
  F. Dad will mop the kitchen floor as needed

8) Other household chores

  A. The cleaning of common areas will be rotated monthly

B. Dusting, sweeping, vacuuming & floor cleaning is needed
   C. Common areas are to be cleaned weekly

9) If friends are coming over, simply let us know in advance; never allow your guest to surprise us.

10) If you are going to be out late, we don't want to be concerned about your safety and well-being after 2 am.

11) If you are leaving on any given day for work, studying, or socializing, all responsibilities noted above must be completed.

12) Other than church, our goal is to have at least one family gathering per week

13) _____, upon full-time employment, you will become immediately responsible for:
   A. Car payment
   B. Car insurance
   C. Vehicle maintenance & gas
   D. Mom & Dad will continue to pay the following until the expiration of this bilateral contractual agreement:
      1. Medical insurance
      2. Dental insurance

14) _____, upon completion of Medical School, this contractual agreement will become null and void and must be re-negotiated if continued residence is desired.

15) _____ & _____ will agree to pay monies already owed that was acquired when both of you became adults & were no longer living at this residence. (See Mom for a detailed report of your invoices owed). Also, tithing is expected.

16) Once residence is re-established at _____, for _____ & _____, any & all unnecessary bills (other than existing monthly) will be repaid immediately upon receipt of your following week's check.

I have read and understand all clauses and provisions contained henceforth. Furthermore, my signature below signifies my concurrence with all clauses and provisions of this bilateral contractual agreement.

_____   _____
Eldest Daughter   (Date)   Youngest Daughter   (Date)

_____   _____
      (**Dad**)   (Date)   (**Mom**)   (Date)

Appendix 2
Fatherhood Interview with Pastor Terrance H. Johnson
Pastor, Higher Dimension Church

Question: Your approach to teaching and preaching the word of God has placed an emphasis on being real and relevant. What advice would you give to a father who has experienced fatherhood out of wedlock?

Pastor J.'s Response: Make an effort not to have sex before marriage. However if you do and a child is conceived make sure you don't outsource the responsibility of being a father. So, whatever it takes in order to establish the relationship and provide resources, do that. Do not neglect that responsibility.

Question: What do you see as the biggest challenge(s) facing fathers today?

Pastor J.'s Response: The biggest challenge for fathers today is not having a father. In early childhood, I remember what helped me to color beautiful pictures was that the picture was outlined so I was able to stay within those lines. Likewise, it's to ones advantage to have a model, someone to trace and see, as an example, to make less mistakes and experience more beautiful outcomes as a father.

Question: I know you are the father of sons and a daughter. Are the challenges of raising a daughter any different from the challenges of raising sons? Please explain.

Pastor J.'s Response: Yes, there are challenges due to the fact that I'm a male and she's a female. However, a lot of challenges are mitigated when her mother is in the home to offer a females perspective, it helps me to father my daughter better.

Question: What role model in the Bible can we look to as a fatherly example?

Pastor J.'s Response: Job is a great example of a father because of three reasons. 1) He prayed for his children that they would accept Christ. 2) He demonstrated leadership in tough times. 3) Despite what he went through he worshipped God. These are three traits every godly father should possess.

Question: **What biblical advice would you share with fathers about parenting in today's society?**

Pastor J.'s Response: The biblical advice I would share with fathers is to train your children to fear God. Make certain you honor God and don't do anything to embarrass your family, be a provider and spend quality time with your children.

Appendix 3
Fatherhood Interview with Aaron Williams, Certified Christian Counselor
The Relationship Coach-
aaronwilliams730@gmail.com

Question: When you became a father for the first time, what was one of your greatest challenges?

Counselor William's Response: As a first-time father, one of my greatest challenges was the fear of failure as a father. Since I did not grow up with my father and I did not have a positive role model in my community as a father, I was afraid that I would impede and limit my children's growth and development.

Question: For the benefit of those fathers who may have experienced brokenness, family dysfunction, or other family-related difficulties during their upbringing, what steps do you recommend in overcoming such pre-parenting experiences?

Counselor William's Response: The 1st step I would recommend in overcoming such pre-parenting experiences is to acknowledge the impact that those past pre-parenting experiences had. The 2nd step I would recommend is to understand and firmly settle in your mind, once and for all, that those past family-related difficulties do not have to predict or determine your success as a parent today. The 3rd step is to take advantage of any and all personal growth opportunities available to develop the knowledge and skills necessary to be the father or parent that you may not have had, so that you can be the parent you desire to be and the parent your children deserve.

Question: What are some of the warning signs (in general) to look for in children where professional counseling may be needed?

Counselor William's Response: Childhood and adolescence can be tough and occasional moodiness is not indicative of an underlying problem and a need for professional counseling. However, if you notice persistent sadness or hopelessness, constant anger or a tendency to overreact in situations, persistent worry, anxiety or fearfulness, difficulty in concentrating or a sudden and unexpected drop in grades; then this is cause for concern. Also, if there is a loss of interest in activities once enjoyed, a desire to be alone rather than in the company of family or friends, unexplained weight loss, and/or substance abuse, then you may want to reach out to the child's primary physician for advice and/or referral for professional counseling.

Question: What would you say to those fathers who may need professional help but are hesitant to seek help because of the negative stigma associated with counseling?

Counselor William's Response: I often smile whenever I am asked this question because I took advantage of so much professional support early in my life that it inspired me to eventually become a professional in this area. I personally experienced the benefits of professional support. The negative stigma associated with counseling is based on ignorance and a misguided belief that I don't need anyone. It's interesting how people, men and women will seek professional support when purchasing homes, cars, boats, vacations, etc. Why wouldn't you seek insight concerning your most valued asset – YOU?

Question: What do you consider to be the key to successful parenting today?

Counselor William's Response: As elementary as it may sound, I consider "responsibility" as the key to successful parenting today. I think that a parent has to feel a deep emotional level of responsibility for their children – the next generation. I think a parent has to know that he or she has a responsibility to develop children who will impact their communities and make a positive contribution to the world by serving humanity. No matter what happens or does not happen within the adult male/female relationship, I believe a parent must feel responsible and to always be in the life of his or her children.

A Quick Review of *Shaping and Sharpening Skills for Your Daughter's Survival and Success.*

Get Started At Birth

Fathers who best create a positive relationship with their daughters start on the day she is born. Get involved in her life from the very beginning.

Take an active role in caring for your baby girl. The more time you spend with her during infancy, the easier it will be to continue building the relationship with her as she matures into a young adult.

Teach Her New Things

While it is great when a father teaches his daughter to ride a bike, **read or do chores**, often the best things he can teach her are life skills." Skills like understanding relationships, money management, career goals, independence, and etc. These skills will serve a girl just as well as a boy and will give her confidence that she can tackle anything.

Just being with her dad, sharing things you are good at will be a real treat for her.

Listen

Many of our daughters love to talk and girls tend to vocalize more than boys do growing up. Knowing this, a father can build his relationship with his daughter by listening more. Pay attention to what she says when you are together. **Listen to what** she is thinking, dreaming and wishing for in her life. And most of all, when information is shared in confidence, make every effort to keep her confidences private. When she shares something with you that is private and bares her soul, don't repeat the story. It is one sure way to hurt your relationship when you violate a trust.

Make Time for Fun

It's important to make father/daughter dates. I suggest checking out the latest toys at the toy store or go out for an ice cream treat. Do things together that are fun and entertaining such as going to the park, feeding the ducks, swimming, going to library, story-time and going to plays. Building fun memories in a positive environment can make a big difference.

Tell Her She's Beautiful

This may sound a little overworked to some fathers, but it is important for your daughter to know she is beautiful. Modern culture and the media often give our daughters messages that they need to be the right weight, wear the right makeup, dress stylishly and emulate models to be beautiful. Teach your daughters self-confidence.

When you tell your daughter she is beautiful, emphasize the importance of being beautiful on the inside as well as the outside. Beauty is so much more than skin-deep. Compliment her often.

Write Notes and Letters

You may remember from your dating years that girls love cards, notes and letters. Take the time to occasionally write your daughter a letter expressing your feelings, letting her know how you feel about her and how proud you are of her. These little **personal expressions** means a lot to our daughters and are a good way of showing love to her.

Be a Great Example of Manhood

The way your daughter sees you treat women makes a big difference in how she will see men later in her life.

Be on your best behavior with her, her mother and other female friends and relatives. Simple courtesy and kindness will go a long way in helping her know what to expect of men in her later life.

Making time and expending energy in building your relationship with your daughter will pay big dividends over time. Even though it may seem as if it's more fun to spend time with the boys, there is still nothing quite like the relationship that can develop between a daughter and her daddy.

Become a Spiritual Example

Don't send her to church; take her to church. Do not allow pride to interfere with expressing vulnerabilities. Don't forget to cover her in prayer.

References and Credits

- American Psychological Association
- Blackdemographics.com
- Bureau of Labor Statistics
- Federal Office of Juvenile Justice and Delinquency Prevention
- National Council on Crime and Delinquency
- National Center for Education Statistics
- Science says parents of successful kids have these 13 things in common Gillett and Drake Baer, Tech Insider Rachel
- The Holy Bible
- U. S Department of Justice Office
- U.S. Justice Programs Bureau
- U.S Justice Statistics
- U.S. Census Bureau
- U.S. Department of Education
- U.S. Department of Justice Profiles of Youth in Custody
- www.fromerostoagape.wordpress.com/2012/08/09/eros-romantic-love-and-agapeunconditional-love/
- www.skillsyouneed.com
- www.totescute.com/four-types-of-love-greek-style/
- www.abundance-and-happiness.com/universal-laws.html
- Www.marketingteacher.com/the-six-living-generations-in-america/Dr. Jill Novak, University of Phoenix, Texas A&M University.
- www.mamalisa.com/What are little girls made of?
- www.today.com/parents/redefining-fatherhood-what-it-means-be-man-today-ds
- www.mnn.com/earth-matters/animals/photos/natures-10-best-animaldads/emperorpenguin
- www.fieldmwuseum.org/science/blog/dedicated-animal-dads-care-theiryoung
- www.mywallpapers.org

- www.successfulstudents.org
- www.bearsmart.com/about-bears/general-characteristics/
- www.alaska-bear-viewing net
- www.abundance-and-happiness.com/universal-laws
- www.allaboutprayer.org/parents-prayerfaqhttp://www.allaboutprayer.org/parentsprayer-faq.htm
- Www.money.usnews.com/529s#grant-low-income-families
- Source Image via ASOC Pictures

Author's Bio

After publishing his first book, *Aspiring Professionals How to Enhance Your Professional Performance and Productivity*, Calvin is proud to release his second publication, **Raising Cougars and Bears (Parenting Daughters – A Father's Perspective).**

Calvin is the father of two young adult daughters. He has 27 years of experience as a fulltime and devoted father. The author grew up in a single parent household in the rural Florida panhandle. Calvin's upbringing lacked having a supportive male family role model. Considering his upbringing, he developed a passion for his life to reflect how overcoming this challenge is possible. Becoming the father of two daughters had a profound effect on him.

The author has had a lifelong fascination with leadership, responsibility, and accountability. This fascination intensified during his twenty-year U.S. Army career. After retiring from the U.S. Army, Calvin went on to a career in Airport Management, culminating as an Operations Unit Manager. After retiring from a successful second career, Calvin shifted his focus to serve in support of several nonprofit organizations where he works as a member of the Board of Directors, Project Manager, and Business Coach. Calvin also takes pride in mentoring young adults, giving back, and drawing from his 33 (+) years of managerial and supervisory experience to help enhance the lives of others.

Calvin has been married to his lovely wife, a professional, independent, and God-fearing woman, for thirty three years. Together, Calvin and his wife are very proud of their daughters. Currently, the eldest daughter is pursuing her Doctorate in Education and the youngest is exploring the possibility of becoming a medical doctor after earning a Master of Science Degree in Biomedical Science.

Please take a moment to check out my first published work, (Aspiring Professionals) How to Enhance Your Professional Performance and Productivity. This publication, along with *Raising Cougars and Bears – A Father's Perspective)* are available at www.createspace.com, Amazon.com, barnesandnoble.com or any outlet where fine books are sold.

If I were to make the statement, "knowledge is power", I am certain that many would whole-heartedly agree. How do you gain this knowledge that results in power? Do you sit back and take a passive approach to gaining knowledge? Or, are you assertive, proactive, ambitious, and serious to seek knowledge and power on your own? This is the dilemma most of us find ourselves in. Read and encourage reading to others. Reading is power!

Made in the USA
Columbia, SC
12 June 2018